HUNGRY TO BE WHOLE

A Therapist's Story of Healing from Anorexia

Brooke Wesley, LSCSW
with
Maureen Rank

HUNGRY TO BE WHOLE

Copyright © 2013 by Brooke Wesley

DEDICATION

I believe that every person that comes across our path serves a purpose. In the decade in which I have been planning this book, I have had the pleasure of learning from the most amazing people. These I've named have served a particularly transformative purpose in mine.

I thank my amazing parents and siblings for their persistence and patience, unconditional love, and commitment to my health. **Mom, Dad, Brynn, Brittancy and Mark,** It is because of you that I am alive to tell my story. You cherish me when I make mistakes and show me my strength as I pick myself up once again.

I thank my husband and children for the allowing me to feel the breathtaking intensity of unconditional love. **Scott, Kendal, Raegan and Corbin**, you are the most precious gifts I could have received, and I thank God every day for placing you in my life. Thank you for taking the journey of life alongside me.

I thank all **my friends and colleagues** for your time, intellect and encouragement.

And, to all of the **individuals** who have joined me in my office, I thank you for allowing me to be a part of your journey to health.

Table of Contents

A Letter from Brooke

Dear Courageous Reader,

Thank you for choosing to share in my story.

Perhaps you chose it because you are struggling with an eating disorder, or because you love someone in the middle of this fight with weight, shape and food. Either way, you've set yourself apart by wanting to learn more, and by determining to make the future a better one.

In the pages ahead, you'll get to know me – an overachieving, perfectionist teenager trying very hard to make life work, and doing it the best way I could: through an unhealthy, but in some ways satisfying, relationship with food, eating and shape.

You'll meet a girl who found that when she focused on clever ways to under-eat and over-exercise, the pain of life seemed to lessen. You'll watch me jump off into a dark chasm, and slowly climb back out.

Then, I want to talk with you from a slightly different view-point.

In the process of recovering from an eating disorder, I became a social worker specializing in helping those who also want life to be different. So, I'll share some of my experiences from the view of a supporter of individuals with eating disorders.

I hope you'll hear the compassion I feel for my those I work with, and how together we honor their willingness to fight for their own lives, even though the fight isn't easy. And I trust that because of the stories I share – my own and others – you'll feel less alone, more normal, less shamed. Perhaps even hopeful.

You may not discover all the answers you seek. But I trust you'll uncover an idea, or a perspective, or a thought that leaves you encouraged and inspired, and more aware of your worth. If any of these things happen because of our time together, your investment will be more than worth it.

PART ONE:

AN EATING DISORDER

AND ME

1

Attention, Please

I started talking when I was but ten months old, and simply did not stop. Not to catch a breath, not to think about an answer before I gave it, and *(God forbid!)* never to give someone else a chance to chime in. Intrusively, insistently, unrelentingly – these were the adverbs attached to my early-emergent verbal skills.

At least this is how my family tells the story, and with probable cause.

When my parents tried to watch television I pushed in with chatter. When they settled in with a book, I asked question after question to pull their attention back to me. When they moved into conversation with one of my siblings, I made myself a part of the word flow, whether the topic was mine to opine about or not.

My intent, of course, was to grab attention. I was out to engage, whether by charm or lack thereof. I was doing something right when others were listening.

About the time I turned two-and-a-half, my family was in an airport, waiting for a flight, and my aunt decided to take me with her while she got a cold drink. As she stepped up to the walk-up bar to order a Shirley Temple, a lady sitting there began to exclaim over me.

"What a darling little girl! Aren't you the cutest thing?" she cooed. But she had made the mistake of offering admiration between bites of the sandwich she was enjoying.

"It is not polite to talk with your mouth full!" I crisply informed her.

To be cute, or to be bossy; both got me attention, and that was enough.

By-passed meant passing out

As early as eighteen months old, I stumbled onto a great attention-seeking technique. In an altercation with my mother over whether or not I would take a bath, I began to cry so hysterically that I hyperventilated myself into passing out. My mother, an emergency room nurse, knew to be very concerned when I began to turn purple. She yelled frantically for my father, and got ready to administer CPR.

Just then I came to.

They were appropriately relieved after such a fright, and held me tightly while they comforted me and each other.

Apparently I knew a good outcome when I saw it. A few months later, another hysterical crying spell led to a blackout, which got me more snuggling and reassurance.

This time my mother sought perspective from her doctor.

"I'm guessing it's a temper tantrum," the doctor told her, "and this is how you'll know. Next time she passes out, don't follow with all that cuddling. Make your response matter-of-fact."

The opportunity to try this intervention came quickly. The family had headed to a mall to rent a tuxedo for my father who was going to a formal party. With the Terrible Twos fully in force, I decided I did not want to be in that clothing store; the "fun" part of the mall should be our destination. I made my preferences known in hysteria that soon progressed to hyperventilation.

"She's going to pass out," my mother told my dad. "Hold her so she doesn't fall and hurt herself." She read me correctly and as my father picked me up, I went unconscious.

But this time, per the doctor's advice, my dad found a quiet corner of the store and laid me on the floor. And when I came to, there was no, "Oh, poor Brookie..." They took me by the hand and led me straight out of the mall to the car. Just as if I had done something wrong! I made my displeasure with this new response clear to all within earshot.

I never passed out like that again. What was the point?

New dramas

I was resourceful; when attempts to provoke my mom into over-attentiveness weren't working well, I decided I might need to call on others for help. My siblings – by this time there were three of us, and soon there would be a fourth – became recruits in my theatrics.

My brother recalls the time I met him as he stumbled half-awake down the hall to breakfast. "Good morning, Dummy!" I greeted him, and promptly punched him in the stomach.

He hadn't provoked me; I wasn't angry with him. I saw a chance to add some action to an otherwise boring start to the day, and I took it.

My parents used to say that even though they had four children, if there was trouble among us, those involved were always "Brooke and…" You could fill in the blank with any of my three siblings; it seemed to matter little to me.

Punishment for bad behavior had some inherent drama; I saw immediate opportunity for upping the ante. As a seven-year-old I once made smarty-flip answers to my mother, so she sent me to my room, underlining her displeasure by a little swat on my bottom as I walked away.

By my reaction, one would have thought I had endured a severe beating. Howls of pain erupted, but Mom wasn't moved and refused to compromise on the time out.

I decided I would have to make it clear that my response was appropriate. So, I actually hit my own bottom several times to redden it well so she would see visual evidence of her meanness. What didn't occur to me was that each time I whacked myself, I left a little kid handprint that provided evidence that the perpetrator of this suffering wasn't my mom.

Life as catastrophe

Not every attention-seeking behavior was as negative. I also tended to annoy by over-caring behaviors.

When I was in late elementary school, my little sister was hospitalized for treatment after an asthma attack. My parents assured us all was well; she was simply getting her body and breathing back in rhythm. Though this explanation reassured my brother and sisters, I would have none of it. I was on them constantly, asking about my sister. What was happening to her? What were they doing to her? Why were my parents keeping me from seeing her? What was going to happen next?

Reasonable information about the hospital's rules, and details about her treatment and her cheery spirit provided no comfort for me. I assaulted her with questions and complaints until she was safely back at home.

However, health issues did provide new material.

About this time I developed a terrible fear of vomiting. My mother thinks this may have come from an episode when, at age three, I swallowed some of my grandfather's heart pills and was taken to an emergency room to have my stomach pumped. Though the medical personnel administered charcoal and other substances meant to induce vomiting, in true Brooke form I simply refused to vomit. After repeated attempts to convince me to "let go," language I still don't enjoy, my mother took me home. However, in the car, the medications took over and I threw up everywhere. All that messiness didn't appeal to me, so escaping it made sense. But as was my way, I took avoidance to the extreme. If anyone in my house were sick, I would confine myself to my room. When I absolutely had to leave, say, to use the bathroom, I would put my hand over my mouth, and run a route through the house that kept me as far away from the sick sibling as possible.

A creative eight-year-old found other ways besides self-imposed isolation to allay her fears of vomiting. When my parents tucked me in, I would look out the window to find the star that shone the brightest, and a ritual would begin. I would say a made-up prayer, then the "Our Father" and then "Now I Lay Me Down to Sleep." I always repeated the same prayers, and always in that order. If I said them right, I convinced myself, no one would get sick that night.

11

Unspoken fears

These prayers must have helped to allay the worst of my anxiety, because I looked for anxiety-reducers for other fears I was embarrassed to admit.

For example, when my parents would leave for the evening, I would slip immediately into terror they would never return. I would sit by the window watching for car lights, praying that each would be my parents returning home in one piece. When my parents returned safely – and they always did – I let out a quiet sigh, secretly praying they would never leave again.

Through this time, I began to react differently to what felt to me like cataclysmic rejection. For example, when my little friend Casey, homebody that she was, decided that she would rather sit quietly watching a movie than come out to play with me, it occurred to me I probably had done something wrong. It wasn't just that she didn't want to play, I told myself; it was that she didn't want to play with *me*. Maybe she never wanted to be my friend again!

I would go to my room, or sit on the front porch and shed rejection tears, or position myself by the dining room window so I could watch for other neighborhood kids coming out to play. Since things were over with Casey, I would have to find others who wanted to be friends.

Red flags or growing pains?

My parents didn't know what to think about these behaviors. They knew we were a normal-enough family. What was up with Brooke? Was she just a brat, as some of their extended family suggested? Or was this just immaturity I would out-grow?

They hoped the solution would come with increased maturity, and looked forward to my start in kindergarten, just ahead. School would give me structure and socialization. Maybe the worst would be over and their attention-insistent daughter would settle in.

School and new behavior

School brought new relationships, and with them, opportunities to forget my own struggles and focus on those around me. The first day of kindergarten I sat beside a little girl with special needs. Knowing she would never be able to enjoy recess like the rest of us, I gave up daily outdoor fun to play inside with her instead.

In a few years, other opportunities to show compassion would arise; among them, a volunteer position at the Rainbow Center for children with special needs. I don't know who benefitted more, these kids who were thrilled to have my attention, or me – a girl with needs of her own that no one seemed to understand.

My benevolent streak continued in later school years, as I became the Good Samaritan for awkward boys. They would hand me a "check yes or no" proposal declaring their undying love, and I would always check "yes," secretly hoping the whole thing would be forgotten amidst the next school-day drama. If one of these notes got out, I would deny it publicly, only to feel sick to my stomach the rest of the day because I couldn't bear to cause others pain.

In other cases, I wasn't quite so sensitive. As our fourth grade teacher handed out spelling tests one day, she asked, "Class, do you have any questions before we begin?" My hand shot up and I replied, "Yes! Mrs. Miller, did you know your bra strap has been showing all morning?" This did not go over well.

"But didn't I just save her from embarrassment?" I remember thinking. "Why was she upset with me?"

A few years later I "saved" another teacher by correcting her grammar in front of the class.

Her response made it clear that I had again crossed a line that I didn't even know existed.

More and more I found myself unsure of boundaries -- caught between the desire to be honest and the fear of going too far.

Fear-driven

By the time I hit sixth grade, fear had become a constant companion – like a familiar face that showed up everywhere I went. The phobia of vomiting escalated, filling what might have been carefree childhood moments with a sense of dread, shame and helplessness.

One day, as I walked home from school with my best friend Tanya, she complained that her stomach felt queasy. As I turned to respond, she doubled over and threw up on the sidewalk. Consumed with fear, I made a beeline for home; I wanted to get as far away as possible from this awful feeling that overtook me.

No sooner had I slammed the door, than the phone rang. "What's the deal?" Tanya scolded, "You just left me there!"

She tried to assure me that the urge to vomit had passed, and she'd just been hungry ("I'm *fine* now!" she coaxed).

However, *I* wasn't fine. And I *wouldn't* be fine until I could hop in the shower and wash away those awful feelings generated by the sight of vomit.

Soon I found myself afraid to fall asleep at night. I developed the idea that people only threw up when they went to sleep, and I would have none of that! Every single night I would do whatever I could to keep my sleepy eyes open. This meant short nights for me, and zero downtime for my parents, who, after doing their best to understand my bizarre behavior, were quickly approaching the end of their rope.

One night they finally laid down the law. No coming out of the bedroom anymore unless something was *really* wrong or unless I absolutely *had* to go to the bathroom. So I hatched a plan: I would head for the bathroom, sit on the toilet, and (since crying to my parents wasn't allowed) I would cry as loudly as possible to God: "God, please let my mommy and daddy know I'm scared. Please send my mommy and daddy to me..." You can imagine the drama a determined sixth-grader could generate with this behavior.

The idea was to let them hear me, and it worked. But they knew they couldn't give in.

Distressed and frustrated, they stood their ground.

My parents weren't the only ones disturbed by these disruptive episodes; my siblings were affected, too. When a brother or sister would vomit, there were automatically two children to care for: the one who was physically sick, and the one who was terribly distressed.

I remember vividly the night I heard my sister getting sick, and immediately ran out of the house into the darkness. Instead of tending to my sweet sister with her head in the toilet, my parents had no choice but to run after me. "This is not okay, Brooke," they said. And I quickly learned what "You're grounded!" meant.

Time for therapy

As confusing as things became, Mom and Dad never gave up; they were determined to help me find a way to normalcy, whatever that looked like. When someone recommended a local therapist, they thought it might promise a new start.

For over a year, I sat across from him, halfheartedly answering questions and wondering when the time would be up. He seemed to try everything, and I made it perfectly clear that I wanted to be anywhere but in that chair.

One day he handed my mother some meditation tapes to play for me when I went to sleep. This sounded like torture, and I quickly stated I wasn't interested. When no one heeded my warning, I found the tapes buried in my mom's bag and destroyed them.

At one point, the flustered therapist called my parents. "The bad news is, you're just going to have to spank your daughter," he told them. "The good news is, her determination will probably make her the president of the United States one day."

They had nothing to say in response. They had been so hopeful he could help, and were starting to feel like they'd exhausted all their options.

New compulsions

The years following were like those arcade games where something pops up and you beat it down with a hammer, only to have another thing pop up elsewhere.

First came babysitting. I decided I would watch as many kids as possible in order to help as many parents as I could. When several calls came in for a Friday night sitter, I wouldn't...*couldn't* say no to any of them.

Sometimes I sat for several families at once, ensuring the parents that, yes, I *wanted* to do this. "The more the merrier!" I would chirp. After all, if *I* didn't do this for them, they'd have no chance of getting a break. It was my responsibility; in my mind, there were no other babysitters in the world.

I remember one family that paid me $1.50 an hour to babysit seven of the most unruly children I had ever met. Still, I would not be deterred from my goal of single-handedly saving the sanity of parents everywhere.

Unrealistic expectations ruled my early teen years, too. I went from being "The Babysitter Who Saved the World" to "Surrogate Supermom" when I appointed myself my sisters' after-school babysitter.

One night a friend called to ask one of them to sleep over. After my sister assured me that she had done her homework and she wouldn't stay up too late, I gave her my permission to go. As she headed upstairs to pack her bag, my parents caught wind of what was going on and quickly overruled my decision.

Somehow during all this caretaking, I finally began to sleep again; perhaps I was exhausted from running the universe! It was a good thing, because my next obsession was something much more active: softball.

My older brother also played, and of *course* I wanted to be just like him. Days spent as a bat girl found me staring longingly at the ball diamond, focusing mostly on home plate, where my brother played catcher. Soon, the fire of overachievement was stoked, and I decided I would become a great catcher, too. I would play every game I could, rain, shine, or sweltering heat.

I was chosen for the All-Star Game most years, and I knew I was a valued player by the way they tried to save me for the tough games (though I insisted I play all of them). And while this newfound ability gave me a sense of importance, it never took away that gnawing feeling that I wasn't *quite* good enough, that if I just tried harder, practiced more, then I would finally "get there."

Uneasiness with a big change ahead

As my parents witnessed all this over-achieving, it's no wonder they were uneasy about what might happen with me down the road. Life would appear to be normalizing; then my over-doing would cause disruption for our family again.

Was I a kid in trouble, or was the therapist's prophecy of a budding United States President going to come true?

"Only time will tell," they told each other. They were more right than they understood.

2

Off the Cliff

The summer before I started high school I hung out with two scrawny neighborhood boys who were impressed with my softball catcher's muscles.

"Brooke, you've gotta flex 'em!" they'd insist. I would laugh and comply, feeling a little embarrassed, but also proud of my strength.

However, when puberty hit, I didn't want to be the muscle-flexing tomboy anymore. The girls in magazines were shaped differently from me, and clearly weighed less than I did. I decided to eat only what Mom prepared for dinner and cut out other meals and snacking.

These changes seemed to be producing results; a nice guy from the next street over asked me to be his girlfriend. "The maga-zines are right," I thought. "Getting attention from boys is better than getting cheered as an athlete, and getting skinnier is getting me more of that attention."

Little did I know that these new priorities for a girl who already unknowingly overdid to get attention meant a perfect storm was brewing.

Longing meets opportunity

During the first semester of my freshman year in high school we were introduced to eating disorders through a movie in health class. I don't recall the ending, but I do recall a girl with anorexia starving herself enough to be hospitalized, then dramatically ripping out her IV's and running away into the night, ending up at home madly exercising and refusing to eat.

This was intended as a warning against destructive behaviors, but that was not the lesson I took away from the movie.

I was intrigued. I had already started eating less, and I knew how to exercise with determination. By doing these things with more intensity, the girl in the movie grew very skinny. Of course getting thin enough to wind up in the hospital wasn't interesting, but looking as thin as she did – what would that be like?

Not long after that, some friends jokingly labeled me as "anorexic" because I stopped eating lunch with them. I would still join the crowd when it came to sharing things like suckers or little candies, but I had decided lunch wasn't an option anymore.

This new label brought mixed feelings – I knew I was being teased and sometimes scolded for my unusual behavior, but I also savored the attention and the new "skinny girl" identity that was rapidly taking shape. I looked more like the models in the magazines; that had to be good. I was avoiding food the way my friends all said they wanted to, but doing it "better" than any of them. If weight loss was a competition, I seemed to be winning.

Real anorexia begins

I didn't know much about eating disorders, but decided I needed to find out more. I began to research anorexia and learned all the signs. Soon, what began as curiosity became a plan of action.

The girl in the movie became my mentor. Besides staying away from food, I discovered the magic of laxatives for a quick "perceived" fix for weight loss, and began abusing them daily. Because I couldn't buy them in front of my parents, I had to steal them. I would make up reasons to go to the grocery store and while there, I would take laxatives off the shelf and hide them away.

Thievery was surprising coming from someone like me -- a rule keeper *par excellence.* I was the girl who fell apart the day I learned my brother had smoked a cigarette. I cried, called my friends, and reacted as if it was the end of the world. When they told me *they'd* tried cigarettes, too, I was devastated.

However, two things were going on: First was my well-established pattern of managing anxiety through compulsive or attention-seeking behaviors. Second was the onset of puberty with its focus on breasts, hips, body shape, body control and sexuality.

Puberty is hard enough for those with *normal* eating habits, but introducing the experience to a person who already struggles with anxiety can create a recipe for disaster.

The year I turned 15, I fell for one of the boys in my neighborhood. One day the phone rang, and my heart did a little flip-flop when I heard his voice on the other end. He invited me to play basketball. However, this innocent game soon turned ugly.

When I asked to use the bathroom in his house, the boy followed me in and started kissing me. With butterflies in my stomach, I found myself kissing him back. But he moved quickly from kissing to touching that first flustered, and then scared me. I asked him to stop, tentatively at first, then repeatedly, and with more force, but he ignored my refusal.

Much later when I would finally talk about this first sexual experience, the therapists surprised me by labeling it "rape."

"It wasn't rape," I corrected her. "He didn't beat me or anything, and I didn't try hard to fight him off."

"Ah, but you refused him repeatedly," the therapist corrected me. "No means no. When a man ignores your refusal, it's rape."

After the experience, I got up and ran home, and took the longest shower of my life. Until later, in therapy, I never told a soul what happened that day.

At the time, I was attending a very fundamentalist church with my girlfriend. When my parents tried to discourage me from going, I played the God card. "It's just church," I protested. "I would think you would want me to go." It was an impressive guilt trip, and they relented, allowing me to attend youth group on Wednesday nights.

I didn't tell them much about what went on there. Each week, the leaders would take us to the basement and ask very personal questions. They'd solicit confessions from anyone who'd had premarital sex, and then insist that in order to be free of these most serious offenses, we'd have to get up in front of the congregation on Sunday and repent.

After the sexual encounter, I was confused and scared -- and now I was also going to hell. In the midst of this, I didn't think I could tell my parents what this church taught. If they stopped me from going, I would lose the opportunity to hang out with my friends. And if they knew the message I was hearing every week, they'd pull me away for sure.

Most importantly, I couldn't tell them about the incident with the neighborhood boy -- not because I was afraid of getting in trouble, but because I was afraid of disappointing them. I had to protect the boy, too. What would people think of him if they knew what he had done? Would they believe me?

So, I shouldered responsibility for my parents' peace of mind, the church's reputation, and a sexual aggressor's community standing while my disordered eating and exercise intensity increased.

Found out

So much was happening so fast; I knew I couldn't keep up the lies I was living with. Then one day in gym class, my behaviors came to light.

When a friend asked if I had gum, I told her to grab it from my bag. My friend found more than just gum in my purse that day; there were multiple packages of laxatives and diuretics – an obvious tip-off to what I had been doing.

And she wasn't the only one who saw.

Each of the girls involved went to different teachers and reported their concern. Over the course of a day, my mother got calls from several teachers, the school counselor and the principal, all saying the same thing: "We are very concerned about Brooke – her friends found her purse stuffed with the signs of eating issues."

Oblivious to the buzz, I headed home that afternoon, hopped off the bus and ran straight for the bathroom – I had taken several laxatives and the need was pressing. On the way, I threw my purse down on the kitchen counter.

Suddenly, from the bathroom, I heard spare change hitting the floor and realized after it was too late my mom was dumping out the contents of my purse.

When I opened the door, laxatives, gum and mints were spread out on the floor.

She shook her head with tears in her eyes, "Sweetie, you can't do this," she said. "We have to get you help."

As I look back, I think I wanted someone to discover what I had been doing. Though my offer to share gum wasn't a conscious cry for help, I allowed myself to get caught. The sexual encounter had happened just a week earlier, and the trauma of that experience had tipped the scales. A delicately-crafted façade could no longer remain.

Two hospitalizations

My parents knew it was time for some serious action, and on March 6, 1992 -- the day after I turned 15 – I was hospitalized for the first time.

I will never forget walking into the inpatient treatment center. The staff examined my luggage carefully, as only non-threatening items were allowed in my room. Bathrooms were locked at all times, meals were monitored very closely and I was in groups almost eight hours a day.

If you had seen me in the hospital that first time, you would never have guessed that I was sick. However, this would soon change. During the week of treatment, the two other patients on the unit proved to be good teachers in unhealthy behaviors. Instead of moving toward recovery, I gained some "effective" tools for being a better anorexic, and I was ready to put them to use.

Returning to school after discharge was as if I had just been treated for pneumonia and everything had been taken care of. My friends said little about the hospitalization, but tried to show support by feeding me: chocolate, pizza, nutty bars. They were determined to help me get better again.

The more they "helped" the more I panicked. I was taking more laxatives in a day than I could count and eating almost nothing. I survived by drinking a full case of diet soda in two weeks and consistently sneaking out after dark to exercise. In the two weeks after my hospitalization, I went from a healthy weight (with unhealthy behaviors) to being significantly underweight.

One night, I slipped out after my parents were asleep and found a park near our home to run. At one point I tripped, slid and fell, severely scraping my hands and arms. However, I got right up and kept on running, oblivious to the spots of blood that soaked through my sleeves.

The next morning, I woke up confused as to how these cuts got there, with vague memories of what had happened, but surprised to see the extent to which I'd been scraped. With the clinical experience I now have, it's clear to me that I must have been experiencing a starvation-induced disconnection from reality, but at the time, I didn't know such things were possible.

This kind of over-exercise was as powerful to me as food denial. For hours every day I would run, do jumping jacks and sit-ups, bicycle, hop on one foot – any movement I could make. When my parents removed all the exercise equipment from the house after my hospitalization, I would find people who were old enough to drive and persuade them to sneak me to the gym so I could use the stair climber.

Within two weeks I was back in the hospital, this time part of a community of women with varied disorders. One struggled with diarexia – she was diagnosed with diabetes, but tried to manage her weight by not taking her insulin. Another had been diagnosed with exercise bulimia. She'd binge, and then get on her Stairmaster for eight to ten hours. (I thought she was the craziest woman I had ever met; she thought the same of me.) Another woman battled compulsive overeating. One girl seemed so young; it was like looking into a mirror. She struggled with bingeing and purging. Most of the women borrowed behaviors from other diagnoses, a condition now known as EDNOS, Eating Disorder Not Otherwise Specified.

Some of the group members would bounce their legs to burn calories during our sessions. Others taught me how to get rid of the meal supplements I was supposed to be drinking by dumping them into various plants. It was a twisted kind of teamwork; they would distract the nurses while I dumped the Ensure.

One night from my hospital bed, I heard a commotion in the hallway. They were admitting a woman with feeding tubes, obviously in crisis. I crept out of bed and watched from my doorway, entering into the anxiety around me as if it were my own.

The next morning I got a look at the newly admitted patient. Amidst a room full of balloons, stuffed animals, flowers and gifts laid a tiny, emaciated figure, the sickest person I had ever seen.

It was a promising national gymnast whose career had been cut short by a debilitating eating disorder. I remember thinking, "That's what anorexia *really* looks like. I don't look *that* bad, and until I do, everyone around me is just overreacting."

I decided in that moment that I wasn't sick. I did what was required to get myself discharged, and quickly reengaged in old behaviors.

By this time, it was May of my freshman year, and my parents had found someone to home school me. Since they still had to work -- insurance wasn't paying for more treatment -- they flew my grandfather up from Florida to feed and watch me during the day.

Time for a new plan of action: I would eat what Grandpa made for me; then I would get rid of it, sometimes by hiding the food in my pockets, sometimes by purging, even though I hated both practices. If my parents had been with me, I would have simply thrown the food back at them. But I couldn't do that with my grandfather.

I continued to deteriorate, with my parents trying everything they could to help. I saw a psychiatrist, a nutritionist, and even a family therapist, but I still refused to eat.

The final hospitalization

Not eating, compulsive exercise, regular purging and overuse of laxatives. My weight was now less than 75% of my ideal body weight.

It had all happened so quickly; in fewer than six months, I changed from a normal appearance to a hollow and lifeless version of myself. Beyond the scrawny, emaciated body, the hair on my head had mostly fallen out. My body had grown a fine layer of fuzzy hair all over; I was freezing all the time – all signs of desperate malnutrition.

At last, my mother could wait no longer for a turnaround on my part; she knew this spiral could well end in my death. So, on my sister's thirteenth birthday, my mother took me to the psychiatrist I had been seeing, and asked for confirmation. Had she correctly read the danger I was facing?

"I agree with your diagnosis," the psychiatrist told her. "It is critical Brooke gets to a hospital today."

"I'll take her to the Emergency Room," Mom told him. "But first we are going home to make my other daughter a birthday dinner. Three hours won't change the outcome for Brooke, but our family's ability to face the future together may. We are going to be a family tonight – Brooke will be part of the family tonight – and we will go ahead together."

When we got home my sister was out by the pool in a lawn chair. I got into the chair with her. We lay there close to each other while I told her how much I loved her, and how sorry I was to cause problems on her birthday. That evening together would mark the end of my life at home for a very long time.

Admission

After the dinner, the cake, the candles and presents, my parents took me to the hospital where my mother worked. Because our psychiatric benefits were gone, she'd arranged for a medical admission from my pediatrician, who admitted me for several weeks.

I was terribly dehydrated and very, very sick. As my dad carried me into the hospital, I asked feebly, "Am I going to die?"

"We won't let you die," he said with more confidence than he felt.

In a week's time my parents negotiated my admittance to a treatment center called Cedar Ridge that was just beginning work with eating disorders. Because our insurance offered no more psychiatric coverage, my dad signed over his retirement funds and I entered treatement. Neither my parents nor I knew what we were getting into. They simply knew my death was not an option. Something had to work.

3

Hitting Bottom

When I was admitted to Cedar Ridge, I came to a world where an eating disorder was considered a life-or-death issue. They took my problem seriously; their policies made sure I did the same.

Eating is not a choice

I was expected to eat *nine* times a day, an insane amount of food for me!

There were no escapes -- no circumventing the rules as I had earlier on the eating disorder units. They insisted on three full meals, three snacks and three health shakes a day.

Plus, these weren't small amounts of food. For example, at breakfast I had to have whole milk, eggs, meat, some kind of carbohydrate, and fruit or juice. An hour and a half later, there'd be a snack like peanut butter on crackers. Then in another hour – a health shake.

If I couldn't finish what they gave me at a meal, that didn't mean the expectations changed. If couldn't complete a meal like breakfast, I would be given a health shake, a snack, and then another health shake within the three-hour period before lunch. Less breakfast just meant more shakes.

Sometimes my stomach would become distended, or I would get sick. But neither of these led to decreased portion sizes. They simply put me on medication to keep my food down. (When individuals now complain that they feel like they're eating all day during this time of re-feeding, I can empathize. I really *was* eating all day, and they probably are too!)

If I was ever tempted to refuse a meal, a feeding tube apparatus waited in my room as a constant reminder of the consequences. I knew that a tube would have been threaded down my nose to force feedings, and if I had pulled it out, I would have been restrained while food was piped in through an incision in my belly button.

Compulsiveness? Not here

I didn't stray from the center's food routine. This, however, didn't mean I let go of compulsive behaviors like exercising. Though I couldn't slip off to a gym like I had at home, I moved as often as I could.

One day a staff member walked in unexpectedly and caught me exercising. I was immediately moved into an all-glass room where I could be monitored 24 hours a day. While using the the bathroom, the only private space I had, a staff member was always present. I had to leave the door cracked and continue talking to them while on the toilet, or changing clothes, or showering so they could hear in my breathing that I wasn't exercising. Someone had rightly guessed I would have been doing jumping jacks any time I could have gotten away with it.

Indeed, they took away *anything* I tried to do excessively.

Once, when I was given a week's worth of homework assignments, I worked through the night to finish them just so I could turn them in the next day. So they took away the homework assignments and I got coloring books instead – at the age of 15!

Another time, they caught me trying to take care of a young boy with developmental delays who'd come to Cedar Ridge, and I was instructed to leave his care to those assigned to him. The lesson was clear: whatever I did to excess was neither appropriate nor acceptable.

Breaking addictive behavior patterns meant withholding whatever we looked to as our "drug of choice." I couldn't play games anymore, and I was rapidly running out of ways to avoid facing my feelings.

The more they challenged me, the closer they nudged me to facing the truth.

"Hey, do your thighs touch yet when you walk?" a nurse asked me one day, knowing that she would provoke discomfort. "Does that question make you mad?" she goaded. "That would make me *really* mad if someone pushed me like I push you."

I thought she was the most obnoxious person I had ever met. However, being mad might mean I would appear less in control, so I smiled sweetly and said, "No, I'm fine; I'm fine."

Once, when I acted out and blew a chance to move to outpatient treatment, a nurse prodded, "Does this piss you off, Brooke? Are you angry?" But I rarely showed distress, proud of my ability to hold my emotions in check. Frustration grew beneath the surface, though, and while I tried to act pleasant, I was increasingly annoyed by their intrusiveness.

Because I had no trust that my body would know what to do with food, I projected this distrust onto the staff. "They just want me to be fat!" I had concluded. When I talked with counselors who'd had eating disorders, I would think, "Yeah,

yeah. They don't know what they are talking about. My body is different."

I wouldn't say it out loud, of course, and in reality they were probably normal in shape and size. However, the distortion in my head was so significant I could see nothing positive about them.

Sharing a dark secret

My days in treatment consisted of therapy and classes: coping skills, boundary setting, social skills and spirituality. I hated the Twelve Step meetings I was required to attend. They were, after all, for addicts -- people with *real* problems. Not me. I would never abuse alcohol or drugs.

I appeared to participate in classes, but I was secretly focused on moving my body the whole time, bouncing my legs, or contracting my booty, whatever might mimic strength training without my being found out. Being preoccupied left no chance for learning how to make healthy choices.

I lived in a constant state of deflection. "It's not really about me; I just want to be skinny." Or, "It's not really about me; I just want to be fit."

At that time, it was believed that eating disorders had some kind of connection to severe sexual trauma. So I was asked repeatedly, "Who has hurt you? Was it your dad? Your uncle?" Immediately, a picture of this boy came to mind, but I was so afraid to point to him, I just stuffed it back down.

I didn't have a history of abuse. But I did begin to wonder if someone had done something to me. Had I missed something? Had something really traumatic happened after all? It was terribly confusing.

Finally about two months in, the story of the sexual encounter just spilled out of my mouth. As I revealed this deep secret, I was surprised that nothing cataclysmic followed the confession. No one rejected me; no one fell apart from the horror of it. Rather than shock or blame, my confession was accepted with quiet acknowledgement and support.

What if this could be true in other places where I felt vulnerable? It was worth a faltering, halting try.

Slowly, more words flowed out. I surprised myself by tentatively admitting I wasn't always happy and sweet and pleasing, that I was embarrassed, guilty and disappointed in myself.

I had decided to try being more honest with people outside my family, though opening up came slowly.

Hitting bottom

A second factor pushed me toward change. At first my family came on every visiting day, but after several months, they had to set boundaries. "We have other children to care for," they explained. "We just can't put our lives on hold, Brooke."

When school started again for my siblings, there would be days when no one showed up for me. My parents honored their commitment to attend every family therapy session, but when visits were optional, they sometimes opted out. They assured me they loved me, and couldn't wait for me to be home, but their always-on-call way of living couldn't continue for the sake of the family.

It was a hard a lesson, but a valuable one. I had experienced gains from my victim status: attention, "specialness" at school, and the constant hovering of family and friends. I had been getting everything I could ask for; why would I *want* get well?

When my family made the decision to shift their focus to my wellness, instead of my illness, I started to change. Eventually, I would hear from my family, "Brooke, you did so well this week and met all your goals! We're going celebrate and take you out to the movies." The rewards began to come for my healthy behaviors, not from my old, sick behaviors.

As hard as it must have been for my family, their decision to stop coming as frequently motivated me to take my own steps toward wellness. They genuinely mattered, and I could see from their choice that if I wanted to be engaged with them, I couldn't continue to be sick.

Four months of gains

Still an inpatient, I wanted to be home again, but to live at home I would have to follow Cedar Ridge rules and maintain 85% of my ideal body weight. If I went below 85%, I would go back to being inpatient.

Finally, one weekend I earned a pass to go home with the agreement that I could move to Day Treatment the following Monday if my weight stayed stable. I eagerly packed my things, anxious and relieved to sleep in my own bed again.

But by Monday I had dropped half a pound.

I went right back to inpatient for another two weeks. No questions. No excuses. No compromise. For someone struggling, a fourth of a pound could mean a return to a death spiral; they were driving home the point that I could not practice destructive behaviors, period.

That moment was a true wake-up call. I couldn't bluff my way through, or smile excessively, or whatever else I had always done to avoid consequences. It became clear that I was not getting out of inpatient treatment until my behaviors changed.

I never dropped below that 85% line again. When I left Cedar Ridge, I had started the process of recovery. I was far from "there," but I was certainly on my way.

Back to school

Life outside of treatment meant learning to live differently.

I had left my school emaciated and I returned weight-restored. But I brought with me a very distorted body image and a lot of discomfort. I wore huge clothes to high school – leggings and big sweaters, for example, because I felt so very fat and unacceptable.

My behaviors had been taken away, but I was left with low self-esteem that was just beginning to push hard into my consciousness. Kids tried to approach me initially, but I didn't feel like I fit in with them.

I coped by seeking out boys to date; there were rarely two days between boyfriends for me. "I must be okay," I would tell myself. "All these boys want to date me." But I was throwing myself into dating relationships to avoid the sadness of not feeling part of a crowd of girlfriends.

Signs of progress

However, opportunities for support came from unexpected places.

When an eating disorder unit came up in health class, I told the teacher the material wasn't right; my experience proved that. She asked if I would be willing to share my story. Soon other teachers were asking me, too. Each semester I would speak to 5 or 6 different health classes about what I had been through.

One night when I was nervous about a speaking engagement the next day, I felt like I wanted to get laxatives. Instead of heading for the store, I called a recovery friend who became my voice of reason. "You have a choice," she said. "You can go get laxatives and not talk tomorrow, or talk and choose against the laxatives. You don't get to do both."

With that challenge, I chose talking.

These experiences of speaking about recovery brought about accountability and distance. The more I told my story, the further away from it I moved. The destructive behaviors slowly became unfortunate memories that no longer had the same hold on my life.

4

The Slow Climb to Recovery

Recovery isn't a once-and-for-all experience. Even if certain behaviors no longer have control, they work hard to find their way into life once again.

As I prepared to head for college, I tried to restrict my eating again, but I just couldn't do it; I lacked the determination to go to my former extremes of starvation. So, I experimented with ephedrine, a "diet aid" that caused me to wake in the night with excruciating chest pains. When I stopped taking it, the experience was as close as I've ever come to drug withdrawal – nausea, horrible headaches and sweating.

After this experiment, I had to accept I now had no options open to me besides eating normally.

No longer over-restricting; now overdoing

My boyfriend and I enrolled at the University of Kansas, and with my signature over-enthusiasm, I began creating a college life. I signed up for 15 credit hours, worked as a nanny two days a week, waitressed at a steak house four nights a week, then added a retail position at a clothing store. I was determined to make enough to cover my car payment, insurance, apartment, and books; three jobs would surely get me there.

Good Girl Brooke was back on the scene.

Enter the Cook

My boyfriend was a very nice guy, but not nearly as motivated as I was. Besides school, he had just *one* job at a pizza joint a few nights a week. He didn't go to class much or get great grades. I would come home and the apartment would be a mess; stacks of dishes and piles of laundry everywhere, so he obviously wasn't spending his time cleaning, either! The contrast between his level of intensity and mine became clearer and clearer.

About this time, a cook at the steakhouse where I worked showed an interest in me. He was ten years older, with a smooth approach to women I hadn't experienced before. And he was just needy enough in the right way to reawaken my "rescue" instinct. I tried to resist him, but he won me over.

I broke up with my boyfriend, started dating the cook, and a few months later he moved in with me.

Soon he proposed; we planned a wedding. He was in and out of jobs so I managed all the bills myself because his credit was poor. However, this seemed to me to be a fixable problem, rescuer that I was.

My family didn't really like him, but they put on the most gorgeous wedding ever. About two weeks before the big day, my mom sat me down to say, "I don't care how much we've spent, or that the invitations have all gone out. If you have any doubts about this marriage, I want you to be able to call it off." Her suggestion offended me. I *was* 21, after all; couldn't I make up my own mind?

The marriage lasted less than 8 months. Even on my honeymoon doubts surfaced as his behaviors toward people we met seemed crude to me. Were there signs of this before our marriage, or was he now simply showing me his true self? Or maybe I was just making too much of a bad day or two.

My doubts multiplied with new discoveries: he was using drugs, indulging in porn and running up bills on phone sex sites. The final blow came after a verbally abusive screaming episode that ended with his punching a hole in the wall.

I left.

It took me two weeks to confess the failure to my parents. "I let you down," I said. "You paid for that beautiful wedding. And I let God down – I'm not supposed to get divorced."

My practical, loving mother said, "Brooke, you are starting your adult life right now. Make sure you've locked every bank account you have. What do you need us to help you with?" (She told me later that when I announced the end of the marriage, she had secretly said, *"Hallelujah!"*)

New direction

A month later, my sister and I moved into an apartment together. I hopped into academic life at a new college with a major in psychology, minor in criminology, ambitiously planning a career as an FBI Profiler. My life was starting again, built around school and overwork at three jobs.

My thoughts about love took a new turn; the idea of healthy boundaries was beginning to take hold. I wrote a list of everything I wanted in a partner – respectful of others, good job, financial stability, a good relationship with his family, non-smoker, no drugs – 30 things in all.

I had come up with these criteria the hard way – through marriage to someone who met none of them. The lesson was a costly one, but I now knew that I could only connect long-term with someone who would respect my boundaries.

When I finished the list, I told everyone I knew I wasn't dating for a year.

However, a few months after the divorce, my timeline was challenged.

During an evening out with friends, I met Scott, who had recently ended a seven-year relationship. Though sparks flew, I told him I wasn't dating anyone for a year because I had just left an abusive relationship. He said, "That's fine. How about if we just hang out for the next 365 days?"

As I got to know Scott, I kept mentally checking off items from my list. He told warm, funny stories about his family; he was motivated and driven; he had a great job…on it went. "He's too good to be true," I thought, "Isn't he?"

When I shared this conclusion with my sister-in-law, she said, "You might be passing up the best thing that's ever going to come your way."

My sister-in-law called it right. Scott did show himself to be the greatest thing that ever happened to me. We were married 14 months after we met.

Boundary setting

Scott was not only healthy, but supported my healthy choices. His affirmation helped me create stronger boundaries with those who'd taken advantage of me in the past.

I had always had girlfriends who I would rescue. One friend had two significant losses in a short time, so I put everything on hold to support her. I rented movies and bought junk food to cheer her up, and held her as she cried. Once I even left a date to listen to her woes as she grieved over a bad haircut.

However, when I left my first marriage, she was nowhere to be found. When I was planning to marry Scott, she turned down an invitation to my bachelorette party, but later in the evening, I ran into her at a dance club. This woman for whom I had put my life on hold was unavailable for me.

After that embarrassing encounter at the dance club, she called to make amends. I didn't respond to her phone calls because I didn't know what to say.

At last I wrote her a letter, detailing all the ways I had reached out to be a friend to her. "But I don't feel this friendship is reciprocal," I wrote. "And I'm not willing to be in a relationship that's not reciprocal."

She called me in tears. "You are so right," she said. "I have not been a good friend. I love you and I want you to be in my life."

This sense of strength grew when the father in the family whose children I had been caring for made a pass at me. I refused his advances, and told him that if anything like this ever happened again, I would tell his wife and leave the job. He waited a couple of months, then tried again.

I called Scott and told him. Instead of being angry or jealous, he said, "You told him if he ever did anything like that again you were leaving. If you continue to stay there he will think your threats are empty."

The next day I told his wife I was leaving; I had set a boundary with her husband, and he hadn't respected it, so I could no longer work there. She was furious *with me* and pushed for details. I said, "Any other questions you have you can ask your husband. He can choose to tell you the truth or lie; you can choose to believe him or not. Do what you need to do to honor yourself."

Setting boundaries with Scott, setting new boundaries with my girlfriend and in a work setting – these successes helped me define myself differently. I loved making people smile, but now I knew I would no longer let myself be used. I had been depleted over and over, and at last, I was learning how to set healthy boundaries.

I was getting better.

Relapse

At this moment in my life, a number of huge changes collided. I had just graduated from college, started my first real job, married the man I had dreamed of, moved into a beautiful new home, and then decided to train for a triathlon.

I had been away from old behaviors long enough that my body felt like it had settled in to "normal," so I didn't see the triathlon decision as being potentially dangerous. But I wasn't able to make up for the energy I was expending in food intake and began to lose weight quickly and dangerously. I dropped to 85% of my ideal body weight.

The weight came off without my really noticing. I wasn't weighing myself anymore so there were no numbers to alert me. My clothes were looser, but they didn't seem dramatically different.

Then I put on the outfit I had chosen for the triathlon, and both Scott and I looked at my reflection in the mirror in amazement – and horror. It absolutely hung on me; the bathing suit looked awful. The next day I went to the gym and hopped on a scale; the truth became clear as I saw those numbers.

When I saw my how much my weight had dropped, I panicked – and began to analyze what I was eating, counting calories, trying to figure out where I had gone wrong. It was a quick return to food focused behaviors in an attempt to make things right.

Putting weight back on should have been simple, I reasoned, but I was wrong. I didn't know how to restore weight by myself. I wasn't taking in enough calories to gain what I needed.

Then, about a month into this experience, I was leading a group with substance abuse people, and my tooth exploded! It literally hit the top of my mouth. This to me was a neon sign of dramatically deteriorating health. My hair started falling out again; my bone structure was so pronounced I looked gaunt and sick.

I needed to help managing my anxiety so I could move toward rest and restoration. I called a nurse practitioner, and went on anti-anxiety medication immediately. I did go back to therapy, but after one session I realized I had not uncovered some new, dark issue: I had simply gotten too comfortable.

It took three months to regain the weight.

That experience brought home to me the realization that the dieting, exercise, and competitive rules others can comfortably live with don't apply to me. I'll never try to run a marathon. I know I could do it, but I won't risk another relapse.

Health matters more.

And my life with Scott matters more. It occurred to me as I recovered that a healthy, vibrant man does not want to be in relationship with someone he has to continually worry about. I thought, "During our first year together we were all over Europe; we were in New York; twice, we went to Colorado mountain-biking. That's the woman he fell in love with, not someone whose weight is too low to enjoy those activities."

I wanted to be that woman once again.

So I now had new resolve. Whatever the eating disorder told me I had gained truly repulsed me. I wanted to be known for health, not illness!

Pregnancy challenges

Now that I was stable in a good marriage, more than anything else I wanted to have children. So, once we felt we were financially secure – I was 25 and he was 28 – we decided to start trying.

I stopped birth control and nothing happened.

Years before, when I was in treatment, people warned that unless I abandoned the behaviors that were part of eating disorders, I would end up with osteoporosis, multiple sclerosis, scarring on my brain, or low calcium levels. Plus, my ability to have babies could be impacted. But I had made fun of what I thought were just scare tactics.

Until now.

At 25 and a normal body weight, I couldn't have a period. After about 12 months of infertility treatments, I started meds to stimulate a period – without results.

More medications and hormones were introduced with no success.

Fortunately, my doctor uncovered a medication intended for people with diabetes that was being applied to infertility. In what I still consider an amazing gift, my body responded to it and I was pregnant soon after starting the medication.

Amidst the joy, I could also see this: many of the dire predictions I had heard about the long-term effects of an eating disorder were coming true. I thought back to the exploding tooth episode during relapse. Also, besides not being able to conceive on my own, I had broken my foot three different times doing nothing more strenuous than walking.

So, I knew then that practices that might work for others – things like dieting or extreme exercise – could never be part of my life. Never. Even if my weight shifted or my clothes didn't fit, the whole diet/exercise fallback I had used before ceased to be an option for me.

My commitment to recovery was cemented.

PART TWO:

A Therapist's Look at Eating Disorders

5

Origins of Eating Disorders

"There's a monster under my bed!"

It's the worried cry of a three-year-old who saw a too-scary movie before bed. And loving parents rush to assure their three-year-old that monsters aren't real.

But those of us who treat eating disorders can tell you monsters are real. They appear in our offices every day, ravaging the lives of beautiful, bright human beings of all ages, all races. (Eating disorders do not discriminate.)

After ten years of providing therapy to those with eating disorders, I've become comfortable with labeling this malady a "monster." Here's why.

About 10-15% of Americans have a diagnosable eating disorder; one in ten of these who struggle are male. This pervasiveness is one of the things that makes eating disorders monstrous.

But it's also the severity of impact that earns it such an ugly label. Eating disorders have the highest mortality rate of any mental health disorder, and the highest suicide rate. Alcohol and other substance abuse disorders are four times more prevalent among those with eating disorders than in the general population.

The monster is a sly one. It often grows in the nicest of families, and takes hold in the brightest and most hard working of young people. Though it often accompanies trauma, those who have never been sexually abused or otherwise traumatized, can still get caught in its grasp.

So, where do eating disorders come from? How do they begin? Therapists usually look toward four contributors for answers: genetics, personality traits, family dynamics, and, of course, trauma.

1. Genetics as a contributor

Nature or nurture? It's one of the most frequent questions I get from families whose daughters or sons are struggling with an eating disorder. "If the answer points to how we parented," they ask, "why is it only affecting one of our children, and not others?"

I wish the answer was simple, and definitive, but it isn't. Research in eating disorders has been minimal so we have much to learn about its origins. But we can say with some certainty that though no clear genetic cause-and-effect for eating disorders has been found, we do know those affected show a greater predisposition to anxiety or depression than does the general population.

A white paper from the University of Maryland Medical Center explains it like this:

"Anorexia is eight times more common in people who have relatives with the disorder. Some doctors believe that genetic factors are the root cause of many cases of eating disorders. Researchers have identified specific chromosomes that may be associated with bulimia and anorexia. In particular, regions on chromosome 10 have been linked to bulimia as well as obesity. Some evidence has reported an association with genetic factors responsible for serotonin, the brain chemical involved with both well-being and appetite. Researchers have also pinpointed certain proteins that may influence an individual's susceptibility to developing an eating disorder."

When we look at family histories, we often find incidence of depression or anxiety, perhaps expressed directly as mental illness, or indirectly through coping mechanisms like drug or alcohol addictions.

When there is a predisposition towards anxiety or depression, the sufferer looks for ways to alleviate these pains, and different outlets work for different people.

The question is: what behavior provides enough of an adrenalin or endorphin rush to distract me from the pain I'm feeling? One girl or boy in a family might find that distraction in an eating disorder, while a sibling utilizes another behavior, like drugs, or relationships, or cutting themselves. The coping mechanism of choice is what seems to fit with the individual make up of each.

Genetics or body chemistry can contribute to the origin of an eating disorder. But we find personality traits to be just as powerful.

2. Personality traits as a contributor

Nearly very personality trait exists among those who suffer with eating disorders, but there is a cluster of traits we see so often in therapy we now label them "the perfect storm."

Most often, we work with young people who show a strong will, an over-eagerness to please, and intelligence – and then a component of self-doubt that generates anxiety. We hear them say, "I want to make everyone happy. I'm going to try to make everyone happy. And if I fail, I am not okay. If others don't like me, I'm not good enough."

Think for a moment about the pressure inherent in what you've just read. *"Make everyone happy?"* Even the Dalai Lama doesn't attempt such a task, yet I have completely sincere 14-year-olds telling me this is their goal.

People pleasing, perfectionism, anxiety or depression, and low self-esteem – these lead to a cycle of avoidance. If you are focused on weight, shape and food, you aren't as engaged in relationship with others, so you don't feel as rejected.

On the other side of avoiding social relationships, eating disorder behaviors can generate compliments, especially when a girl begins to drop weight. "I just wish I had that will power," she'll hear. And she'll tell herself, "This must be working. I'm eating less and becoming more pleasing to others."

It's this imbalance that seems to take hold in some personalities very early.

In very young children we see it expressed sometimes in tantrums or raging.

Older children express it differently. Like the fourth grader who says to herself, "My teacher doesn't like me. I've had other teachers who liked me, but this one I can't win over, no matter what I do. There must be something wrong with me." When these feelings are held inside, then coping skills to help bear the weight of negativity begin to emerge.

One young person told me, "I began to feel uncomfortable with my body in third or fourth grade. I noticed I looked different than other people." And thus began the start of behaviors that would grow into a full-blown eating disorder.

However, most food-related coping mechanisms – and especially anorexia – usually start around the onset of puberty. As bodies and hormones begin to shift, uncomfortable emotions surface. Current research suggests 85-90% of girls in junior high and high school have tried to diet. And of that 90%, nine will end up with an eating disorder.

Why are some more driven, and others not? We don't know, but we do know that when we see highly driven, perfectionist, approval-seeking traits, an eating disorder might be ahead.

3. Family dynamics as a contributor

Let me be clear: the majority of parents I work with are supportive, loving people who are dumbstruck that their beautiful, athletic, highly-competitive, smart child now weighs 87 pounds and is struggling for her life against an eating disorder.

"What happened?" they ask me. "What did we do wrong?"

For some, the "what went wrong" has less to do with them and more to do with genetic tendencies and cultural pressure that their offspring dealt with in an unhealthy manner.

But for some, parental pressure does play a role in the development of a child's eating disorder. In some cases, it's the family's rigidity, or unrealistic expectations, or comparison between siblings that contributes.

Parents can have their own issues with perfectionism. For example, "If my child doesn't get her homework done, it's going to reflect on me."

One father I worked with showed these perfectionism pressures clearly. As the owner of his own company, he worked incessantly – but also talked and pushed incessantly, nearly to the point of mania. Mom is equally high performing – a successful businesswoman and philanthropist.

To this twosome is born a daughter who tells me she is terrified of not measuring up to her parents' expectations. She's terrified the treatment they've just paid for is going to be wasted because she's not doing better. "I failed them," she confesses to me.

But I can see her image of the two perfect people who parented her likely is more nuanced than it appears. Her father's brother and his father are both alcoholics – signs of a pattern of dysfunctional coping that might be part of this family's heritage. Mom brings her own set of issues. She reports her sister struggles with depression to the point of requiring hospitalization.

With these parents, the bar for health is very high: their daughter is sick or she's not. It's black or white. There's no room for learning, growing, progressing, even if the progress is slow. The girl who used to purge six times a day now purges only six times a week. How remarkable this is!

"But I'm still a failure," she tells me. "I'm still purging."

"You are," I respond, "but only a fourth as much as you were. That's worth celebrating!" But she's not convinced, because her parents aren't.

When parental pressure is well-intentioned

Some parents I work with aren't pushing their children to meet the parents' needs; they push to protect their child from the consequences – and pain – of not succeeding. But this approach often backfires in ways parents wouldn't expect.

When kids don't make an athletic team, for example, you'll hear, "It isn't because my kid lacks ability; the team selection process is based on politics, not skill!" And calls go out to the athletic director.

If a child isn't on the team, he or she may feel disappointment – but a win could also result if parents say, "There's always going to be someone better than us at everything. Let's practice and show 'em next year!" But a too-protective parent can actually create a loss with their full-court press to secure their child's spot on the team.

I've had young people tell me, "My dad got me on the team, but I figured that if he had to fight that hard for me, he must believe I can't make it on my own. I guess I'm not good

enough, so I've got to perform better than everybody else to
show them I belong. And I have to always be happy because
I'm starting as the outcast who didn't earn a place like the
others."

When kids create parental pressure

There are those who push their expectations of themselves onto
their parents. I think of one young woman who talked to me
about what she feared.

"I'm afraid of getting anything below an A on my report card,"
she began. "And I'm afraid I won't make the varsity cheerlead-
ing squad…or get fat…or have people be dissatisfied with me.
Being injured scares me – because that would lead to getting
fat and not being able to perform."

And so it went. But as I got to know her family, it seemed
clear her parents weren't pushing these expectations. They
came from some complex combination of anxiety, personality
and culture. However, attributing her heightened expectations
to her parents helped release some small bit of pressure; it
provided a way to say, "It's not all my fault that I'm struggling
like this!"

Parental pressure can contribute to eating disorders, but careful information-collection needs to happen before we rush to judgment.

4. Trauma as a contributor

At least half of those I work with have been exposed to trauma. The most common is sexual trauma.

I think of the young woman whose experience with molestation began at her stepfather's hand when she was three, and continued through her eighth year. And beyond the sexual invasion, the psychological abuse perpetrated by her stepfather was almost unbelievable.

Time and time again she reported and over and over the adults in her life let her down. She began to dismiss the people around her – and rightfully so – but she also came to believe that she couldn't trust her own instincts.

By the age of nine she started throwing up. Mom at last believed her story, and divorced the stepdad, but by then the damage was done.

Think with me for a moment about what this little girl learned in these episodes. First, she clearly cannot trust her own instincts. "This man is coming in my room," she tells herself. "He's supposed to love and take care of me. My mom loves him; my brothers and sister love him. But he is hurting me, so I must be doing something wrong."

Every message confirms to her that she must be unlovable. "I thought I was okay, but the way he's hurting me tells me I'm not. And if my mom doesn't protect me, I must not be okay."

Eating disorders can serve as a very superficial mask. What to do with all these secrets? Then begins restricted eating and starvation. Or perhaps bingeing and purging to fill the emotional hole.

For this young woman, the hole felt like a bottomless pit. There was nothing she could do to repair the hurt. The only way to find relief in the moment was to instead feel hunger pains, or be so exhausted from exercise that her ears felt bubbly and her mouth dry. Now, instead of struggling with the trauma, she can hyper-focus on weight, shape and food. Food, or the lack of it, becomes a magnificent distraction.

Trauma comes in different sizes

I've found it useful to understand the difference in what Dr. Kim Dennis calls *Big T* and *little t* traumas. Extended sexual abuse is a *Big T* trauma. The horror one young woman suffered at age 8 when her father died of a heart attack before her eyes as he drove her home from school was a *Big T* trauma. Abuse or neglect are other examples.

Little t traumas could be an accumulation of real or perceived rejections. One episode might not constitute a trauma, but the collection of many episodes over time can generate trauma responses as destructive as do the *Big T's*.

Highly anxious and sensitive young people can traumatize themselves by repeatedly interpreting daily ups and downs as rejections. What others might process as "life as usual" feels larger, hurts deeper to these kids. And putting a cluster of these ups and downs together moves them to generate trauma-based approaches to cope with life that distract them from the pain they feel. Approaches like eating disorders.

Origins point us to a battle plan

What does it matter how the eating disorder began?

We investigate not to place blame, but rather as a starting point to target the best ways to assist individuals and their families toward recovery that lasts.

Now that we've asked questions about where the monster came from, we're ready to confront him by getting smarter about how he presents himself – knowing the red flags of eating disorders - and by knowing how to seek the best fit in treatment approaches.

Confrontation lies ahead.

6

Warning Signs and Treatment Directions

We've all seen the photos the skeletal waif with bones protruding. So, identifying someone who struggles with an eating disorder is fairly straightforward. Right?

Actually, it's not. You may be surprised to learn some of the indicators may be right in front of you, but not behaviors you've tied to eating disorders.

Red flags

When a person struggles with anorexia, he or she may focus on choosing very low calorie, high protein meals, then throw most of it away. You may also notice frequent bathroom stops during the day. These are required because of fluid loading – drinking a lot of water, perhaps – to keep flushing fat from the system. Or you might notice constant movement, like knee-bouncing, even when you'd expect quiet.

When my own anorexia was at its height, , I would leave every class every day to run the steps when no one was in the halls at school. If you have to keep moving to keep weight coming off, but there's no way to get outside or get to a gym, you get creative!

Bulimia can generate frequent bathroom trips, too, but especially after meal or snack times, to purge. And you may notice lots of water or milk consumed with meals since heavy liquid intake helps the purging process.

In the early stages of bulimia, teeth marks can show up on girls' hands, especially about an inch above the wrist. Shoving a hand far enough down the throat to induce vomiting can leave teeth calluses or even light scarring. Also, continual vomiting can cause swelling in the parotid glands just under the chin line, so the girl may take on a "chipmunk jaw line" look.

The use of laxatives in either disorder will necessitate numerous bathroom stops during the day. And talking from a dehydrated condition makes the lips sound sticky. Or you may see goop or residue on the sides of the mouth, again, from dehydration. Friends will notice the continual use of gum, mints, suckers, anything to give a sense of flavor without consuming calories.

You'll also see food being cut into many tiny pieces, as if a two-year-old is eating from the plate. Pushing the food around on the plate to avoid consuming it, excuses to miss meals – both are covers for not eating. You also may no longer see foods in the pantry no longer being eaten. Or perhaps they are disappearing far too rapidly. If a whole bag of Oreos is gone in a day, for example, I would want to know why. Bingeing could be going on, or else overeating, and then purging.

Thinness as a red flag?

Surprisingly, people with eating disorders don't always look skeletal. Even with bingeing and purging, it's only possible to dislodge about two-thirds of what's in the stomach. If a girl stuffs herself on 4,000 calories – a small pizza, a gallon of ice cream, and maybe a sleeve of chocolate chip cookies, then drinks milk to prepare for the purge, she may still be left with an intake of more than 1,500 calories. Even though she's purging, she may still maintain or gain weight.

Over time she may move to purging after every meal to make room for another binge, and then go on to bingeing and purging several times a day. When the disorder reaches this point, pounds may begin to come off.

It also seems that the body is incredibly adaptable. I've seen males and females who are consuming amazingly small amounts of food whose metabolisms seem to keep slowing down to accommodate. Their bodies hold onto fat reserves with determination, so weight loss may not show itself in a way that correctly represents the very small amounts of food they are taking in.

I frequently hear parents say, "My daughter is gaining weight – she can't have an eating disorder."

I work immediately to refocus their attention. "How much time every day does she spend thinking about weight, shape and food?" I ask them. Instead of weight loss, a more correct indictor is a hyper focus on body issues, and micromanagement of their intake in ways that are neither healthy nor balanced.

Body checking or body avoiding

Eating disorders lead girls to be overly aware of the size of their body parts, so you may observe body checking consistently throughout the day.

Body checking means playing with rings to be sure they can still move freely on the fingers, rubbing their collar bones to be sure their bones are still protruding, running hands over the stomach to assure pants are big enough and their hip bones are easy to locate, or wrist-checking to be sure they can still fit their fingers around the wrist.

A few weeks ago I was changing clothes in the locker room at my gym, and noticed another woman without clothes walking up to the mirror to check out her behind. Then she put on her panties, walked back to the mirror and checked her behind again, as if the addition of underwear would cause some change. And again, when she put on her jeans, it was back to the mirror for a third check.

Individuals I work with check over and over whether their stomach is flat, or if there is still enough space between their legs to keep their thighs from touching. You might even find them in public restrooms standing on the toilet to get a full body view in the mirror.

The other side of body checking is body avoiding. I see it in the person who walks into my building and takes great care not to catch a glimpse of his reflection in the entryway windows. Or in hallways he'll make sure to turn away from mirrors. Or in therapy he'll sit on the couch, and immediately try to cover himself with the throw pillows. Other times, individuals might wear a winter coat to – and through – every appointment for an extended period, or show up in a baggy sweatshirt, even though the weather is warm.

Challenges in diagnosis

We've talked about some of red flags that might suggest an eating disorder. However, seeing these red flags can be challenging for three reasons: the innate secrecy that goes with this illness, the cultural "approval" of unhealthy behaviors, and the propensity to disbelief on the part of parents.

1. The challenge of secrecy

People with bulimia usually aren't bingeing and purging in the presence of others, so it's hard to get a sense of what's going on. It may happen in the middle of the night, or when no one is at home. Or the person who is struggling may be frequenting a drive-through restaurant to load up on food, then using a gas station restroom to purge.

Many families tell me, "We can't believe we missed this!"

"Of course you missed it," I tell them. "If your child is purging and doesn't want to stop, she's certainly not going to announce the behavior to you." To many, these behaviors are very embarrassing to admit. I frequently hear, "This is so disgusting! I would never want anyone to know I'm doing this; it is just gross!"

2. The challenge of cultural support

When over-exercise takes place, we tend to say, "Gosh, I wish I had the stamina to do that!" Or with reduced eating, we respond, "Wow. You have so much willpower!" We live in a culture where these behaviors are applauded, even held up as examples to others.

Some individuals hear, "You must be naturally thin." I tell them, "Honestly, no one is that naturally thin. Our bodies aren't built to look emaciated. Those who do are either have an eating disorder or some other illness."

3. The challenge of parental disbelief

If you've never struggled with an eating disorder, it's easy to think, "Why can't you just sit down and eat your lunch?" These behaviors make no sense to people who have never wrestled with food obsessions. I continually work to try to help parents understand – and to believe what's really happening to their child.

One father told me proudly, "I think my daughter's doing well. I took her to Cheeseburger in Paradise last Thursday and she ordered a burger and fries – even a soda!"

He provided this report me to the following Tuesday. "So, great," I responded. "Did she eat the next day? We need more than one meal to correct this behavior, and it's been five days since Cheeseburger in Paradise."

"Well…" he stumbled, "I *feel* like she's probably doing okay."

When we weighed his daughter, she was down a pound.

When families prefer to see an eating disorder as "no big deal," they'll get great support from their daughter or son, who would prefer to agree it's no big deal and keep on with unhealthy behaviors.

I asked one mom to document her son's food intake. When I saw her nine days later, she came to the appointment with only three days' documentation. "I've been out of town on business," she explained, "and I didn't want to bother his stepdad with this food record business."

I wondered if her son had needed daily medication for a life-threatening disease, whether or not she'd ask her husband to help administer meds. If in that scenario, she still didn't want to bother him with her son's needs, there are family issues present a simple encouragement to diligence won't help.

But more commonly, the need to uncover and create accountability for eating disorder behaviors isn't taken seriously until a health crisis presents itself.

Finding a treatment partner

Increased chances for recovery lie in connecting to the right resources for treatment. I got help at a substance abuse treatment center, but I've come to believe after treating hundreds of people, that the best shot at recovery comes through work with a treatment team who is particularly trained in this area.

There are two reasons why.

First, the all-or-nothing, pass-fail recovery model isn't a good fit.

In treating eating disorders, the outcome we seek is balance. Those treating alcohol or drug issues don't intend to help people become more balanced in their use of cocaine, for instance, but rather to withdraw from it completely.

In substance abuse, the thought process to recovery is of necessity black-and-white. That's why someone who struggles with alcoholism might announce she has had eight months of sobriety, or a drug user might declare himself "clean for two years."

But for those in the eating disorder world, black-and-white thinking is a stumbling block to recovery, and emphasizing it sets them up for failure. Many already live in an either/or world: I'm good or I'm bad, I'm sick or I'm well – there is no in-between. Our job as treaters is to help them replace the "or" with "and."

Eating disorders sufferers desperately need to learn to move in a world of grays. There is no Valedictorian of Recovery from Eating Disorders. Those engaging in treatment are on the way; all are in the process of growing, learning, and stepping little by little toward better choices, better health.

And recovery from an eating disorder usually means one step forward, one step back, one to the left, three to the right. It simply isn't a ladder to climb or a set of boxes to check. Ambivalence is a necessary part of learning.

For instance, one step in recovery has to do with releasing the scale. In eating disorder, the scale can be a trigger for obsessive behavior – and in response, struggles find themselves weighing multiple times a day, or before and after every workout, even before and after a trip to the bathroom.

Some use the scales as a mood determinant. If I weigh in at 138, then go work out and reweigh at 136, I'm jubilant. And I'm reinforced in thinking that the more I work out, the less I'm sure to weigh. But if I work out, and then weigh in at 141, I collapse emotionally. So besides losing joy, I again decide more extended workouts are in order to take off what I inexplicable gained. It's a no-win. The eating disorder is validated either way.

But when I ask individuals to let go of the scales, they sometimes wind up recovering them – even buying another! If this happens, we don't consider it failure, but rather a chance to learn. We look at how long they went without the scales and how they coped without it. If they'd been weighing themselves 14 times a day, then went for nine days without weighing, that's progress! That's positive movement.

I consider these steps learning, not success vs. failure. In treating the perfectionism that often accompanies eating disorders, this thinking shift can be critical.

Second, behaviors can be easy to miss.

One young woman announced proudly that she had eaten breakfast before she saw me that day. She had previously been a breakfast skipper, but because I know eating disorders, I gave her no gold star. Instead, I asked questions.

"What did you have for breakfast?" I queried. Turns out it was Special K waffles.

I perked up. Special K is classified as a "safer" food by those with eating disorders – high in protein, low in calories and fat, so if one has to eat something, there is less chance of weight gain with Special K.

"What about those Special K waffles was appealing to you?" I asked.

"Oh, they just looked good," she responded quickly.

"Did the waffles look good?" I pushed, "Or the box?"

Turned out it was the box that held appeal. And not the picture of the waffles on the front – but the calorie count on the side. And as she admitted to calorie-checking, she laughed out loud. I had found her out! The waffles weren't intended as a step toward balance; they were a way to appease those who were trying to squash her behaviors while keeping her weight low.

Or listen to this interaction with a woman who told me firmly she ate really, really healthy and exercised moderately.

Hmmm. I pursued. "What does eating healthy mean to you? And exercising moderately?"

This young woman said, "I reduce my carbs and fat, and never exceed 1200 calories a day." Without eating disorder awareness, it's tempting to think, "Gee. I wish I had that kind of discipline," instead of asking, "1200 calories. How is that eating well?

As for exercising moderately, this young woman told me upon questioning that she worked out seven days a week, two-and-a-half hours at a time.

"What happens if you miss a day?" I asked.

"Oh, I don't miss."

"But what if you did miss?

"Gosh. I don't know. I've never tried it. Actually, I can't miss."

On the question of purging, individuals may tell me they are not throwing up. But I know that definition may mask a whole variety of behaviors. I ask about diuretics, laxatives, and ephedrine pills. Or whether they've gotten a prescription for Vyvanse or Adderall, both stimulants that increase weight loss. And I of course ask about over-exercising – there are many ways to purge calories.

Questioning like this exposes behaviors, but when behaviors such as limited eating or extensive exercise are socially attractive, those without specific training in eating disorders may miss important data points and slow the road to recovery.

How to look for a treatment partner

If the internet is your starting point – and it is for many – there is a marketing insight that will help in directing you. Websites, or therapist referral sites, can sometimes mislead. When professionals like me register for or create these sites, we are often offered a menu of offered services from which to choose. Picture a list of disorders one might treat, with boxes to check beside each one. Typically "eating disorders" is always one of the items on the list of options.

So, because therapists pop up in a web search as treating eating disorders, it doesn't necessarily mean they have specialized training. Some professionals without focused training check this box because they assume the general approaches they use –

like cognitive behavioral therapy, for instance – can be applied to this challenge, too. Of course it's to a professional's marketing advantage to check as many boxes as possible, since this increases the pool of potential clients.

Instead of simply selecting anyone who lists "eating disorders" as a treatment area, I'd suggest you ask these two questions:

First, what has their experience been in treating eating disorders? I'd want to know that 50% or more of the people they treat come with this diagnosis.

Second, what is their specific training in treating eating disorders? You'd want to hear they've attended some of the major eating disorders symposiums held regularly around the country to stay current on continuing education and reseracrh involving the world of eating disorders.

Third, it's also helpful if you find a practice that specializes in treating eating disorders. This means you'll be working with a therapist whose colleagues are immersed daily in hearing the stories and working with behaviors specific to anorexia or bulimia. Those with time and experience in this space are tougher to fool – and that will be to your advantage. They also have interventions and support ideas that come from continual conversations with individuals and other professionals.

Last, look for a sense of trust because the trust factor weighs heavily in successful therapy. If after five or six sessions, there isn't the sense that the therapist can receive secrets, a shift to another therapist might be in order.

But I add one caveat. Few feel trust in the first session, or the second, or sometimes even the fifth! Trust doesn't come in a heartbeat, especially when we are attempting to eliminate a disorder that many people feel is their identity. However, the question of trust must be answered satisfactorily at some point for therapy to be effective.

What to expect during treatment

As you begin the journey to recovery, it helps to understand how a therapist specializing in treatment of eating disorders sees the process. I use a three-step protocol.

Phase One

I begin with **basics**, checking for nutritional deficiencies though lab work ordered by a primary care physician, determining what behaviors need to get under control at once, and deciding if a structured eating experience needs to take place to get weight up.

This first diagnostic step focuses on severity and safety. Can the work ahead begin in an outpatient setting, like my office, or is an inpatient treatment plan the best option? A team approach is key. If we choose outpatient treatment, a nutritionist, a primary care physician, a psychiatrist and family therapist may all be called upon as team members.

Phase Two

Next I move to **relapse prevention skills**. Once we've begun to change dangerous behaviors, how do we keep this work going? What triggers do we need to identify? What redirection can we incorporate as coping mechanisms?

Here my intention is re-equipping the person with new skills and responses to meet pressure situations and disturbing emotions without resorting to old behaviors.

Here are examples.

One of our early relapse preventers might be journaling. But a move to journal feelings rather than purge in a big challenge. So, I might encourage an individual to post notes is regularly visible places, like the bathroom mirror, that remind her to go first to writing her feelings before she choose more destructive behaviors.

With others who demonstrate obsessions about eating, calories, and exercise, I might suggest adopting activities that require hand-eye coordination, like building a house of cards, or puzzles, or Sudoku. Activities like these require involvement from both sides of the brain, taking away "mental room" for obsessing about calories consumed.

Interventions like these require training, because even though other kinds of distractions, like television, reading or listening to music, seem reasonable, they don't work to break obsessive thought patterns. They are simply too passive, from a brain engagement perspective. They don't work to push the brain retraining that generates new, healthier neural pathways.

In this phase of therapy, our intent is to help turn the corner from illness toward health so a future-focus toward living strong can begin.

Phase Three

The third phase of treatment moves to re-building. Here we work on **life issues**, facing the emotions the eating disorder has been covering.

One individual in the life issues stage popped into my office announcing her boss had been rude that day; she was going to quit her job.

As we explored what had actually happened in the exchange with her boss, it became clear that she had not told her boss how the admonition she had received had frightened and embarrassed her.

As we explored what it might look like to talk to her boss, the woman said, "I'm going to say, 'I know you have a problem with me!'"

"Where would that get you?" I asked. She admitted it would likely make her boss angry. So, we explored a different way to communicate what she needed.

When the time came, the young women was able to tell her boss, "I feel you are upset with me and I don't understand why." Her boss was astonished, and apologized, then said, "If I ever get in that mood again, let me know, because I had no idea I was coming across with such harshness."

Communication skills are part of life issues. As we work together to find other ways to do life, the likelihood of eating disordered behaviors resurfacing begins to diminish.

Sometimes work on relationships moves toward more intimate issues. One woman talked about her concern that during the past three months, her husband had been gone from home nearly every weekend. This change in behavior generated fears that he might be having an affair. The temptation to respond with old behaviors was strong.

We worked together on a new approach: confronting him with his behavior change, and talking to him about her fears. Preparing for this conversation was a major learning process, since she had become skilled at avoiding these feelings of fear. But as she courageously introduced this difficult conversation, she learned there was no affair. However, he was escaping what was for him an uncomfortable change in their life together.

Now the focus could shift from a fear-based imaginary issue to a real issue about their closeness. They needed to now work together on how to find each other in this new relational space.

Another young woman felt anxiety about visiting her dad's house because of discomfort with his new wife. The black-and-white, all-or-nothing thinking so typical of an eating disorder told her she either had to be miserable visiting at his house, or give up seeing him completely. Neither felt good.

In life skills work, we thought instead about some "what about" scenarios. What if they still met, but just not at his house for overnights? Could going for ice cream be an option? Or attending a ball game together? Or going for bike rides?

Our work together was about much more than solving a visitation problem. We were working to create new, and more flexible problem-solving skills that might ease the challenges of living in the world.

Treatment is a partnership

If I could gift the individuals I work with one major thinking change, it would be this: You do not have do this alone!

Eating disorders are isolating. Plus, the thought patterns that drive them emphasize perfection, so a struggler feels a double failure in disclosure. He or she has failed at maintaining health, and then failed to maintain an image of perfection to others. The way out can feel very lonely.

Families can feel isolated, too, as others without understanding tell them, "Why don't you just make her eat?"

Good treatment partners confront isolation. A positive therapeutic match will increase the chances you'll feel that you are no longer alone, and no longer hopeless. There is life beyond an eating disorder; a professional with specialized training and a capacity to build trust can help you find it.

7

New Ways of Living

As you know from my personal story, those with eating
disorders sometimes bury their pain inside the pain of others
they are determined to rescue.

Leaving this behavior doesn't always come easily.

In the same way, even though eating disorders can create life-
threatening havoc, leaving them can feel as traumatic as a
romantic break-up. That's why our approach to treatment
readiness starts with crafting an end – and then building several
new beginnings.

Breaking up – even with an eating disorder – is hard to do

Individuals are often surprised by the way we begin our
relationship, especially when I ask them to tell me about the
pros and cons of their eating disorder. They expect to talk
about how it has hurt them. What they rarely expect is a
conversation about how it served them at some point.

No part of life is completely good or completely bad. And I believe we pursue behaviors that may become destructive, not always because we are bent on self-destruction, but because these behaviors provide some gain others fail to understand. For example, eating disorders can give an intense, ready distraction from the pain of trauma, loneliness, worthlessness, or anxiety. Those are gains, indeed.

Readiness for a real break-up comes when we honor the parts of the behaviors that proved helpful, while we acknowledge the disruption and pain those same behaviors created.

That's why early in our time together, I guide people in crafting a "Dear John" letter to anorexia or bulimia, or whatever name they give to their out-of-balance relationship with weight, shape and food. In the letter, they acknowledge the help they've received from the disorder, and then delineate the disruptions that are leading to this break-up.

From this separation, we are ready to begin the exploration and application of new skills based on health and worth.

Confronting false perceptions

A young girl in the throes of anorexia insisted to me that she had to keep losing until her weight was in the double digits – in other words, 99 pounds or fewer. Then, and only then, she'd be happier.

"Let me get this straight," I said. "Do you feel happier than you did a couple of months ago? I'm asking because in that time you've lost about sixteen pounds. Doesn't each pound lost make you just a little happier?"

"It doesn't work like that," she said. "I won't be happier until I'm thin, and I won't be thin until I'm 99."

With body image, it's as though we make imprints on our brain that reach near-permanence. One 23-year-old woman swears to me that because she's now eating instead of starving, her body is growing by leaps and bounds. In reality, she's lost weight. But I believe when she looks at herself, she honestly sees a fuller-figured girl than she saw a few weeks ago.

With the distorted thinking that accompanies eating disorders, ideas we actually know can't be true sometimes *feel* so true that we believe them.

Early in my anorexic period, my sister touched me with ranch dressing on her hand. I was so convinced that the fat from that dressing would seep through my skin and deposit on my hind end that I scrubbed my arm until it bled.

I thought of my odd behavior as I reflected on the conversation with this brilliant young woman. Even though I could see the change in her appearance as sixteen pounds fell from her body, she absolutely could not. When she looked in the mirror, all she could see was the girl she was sixteen pounds ago.

One young man who'd lost considerable weight told me, "It's funny that my clothes are now too big for me. When I have my clothes off, my body looks just the same as it used to. All I can figure is my clothes have stretched out somehow; maybe I'll wash them to shrink them back to size."

These imprinted perceptions are tough to change. However, once breakthroughs occur, and new, healthier perceptions get a chance to imprint, these can be equally sticky. That's the hope in treatment. So much of our work involves surfacing thoughts and perceptions that lead to illness, and replacing them with life-giving perceptions.

An early perception-exchange process like this usually centers on the issue of self-esteem.

Self-worth and self-esteem

I'm not one to spend precious therapy time helping people improve their self-esteem.

What? What did she say?

You heard me. And yes, I know the popular assumption that if individuals with eating disorders could only salvage their flagging self-esteem, they'd stop hurting themselves and get well.

People I work with largely agree. I heard from one recently who said, "Low self-esteem is my big problem, which is why I need to be skinny. Skinny means pretty, and pretty means more people will like me. I'll get more attention. And with more attention I'll get a better job...I'll get a better husband..."

Whoa. Those "good self-esteem" behaviors she just rattled off to me quite likely aren't going to happen as she hopes. So, then what? If being okay depends on getting every action perfect, and being what everyone else wants us to be, we can count on never being okay.

I prefer to approach the path to being okay from a different starting place, not by focusing on self-esteem, but rather by understanding self-worth.

I ask these questions: "What if you were valuable, just because you're here, just because you're human and alive? And what if you were intrinsically as valuable as anyone else, or everyone else? How would you be different?"

I ask because in the end, I believe these are the questions that bring positive change to these struggling young women and men I sit with every day. They do things wrong; they try and fail. And they are convinced they can't have value until these failures are behind them.

Because of black-and-white thinking, failures don't mean they're a little unworthy; they are completely unworthy, and it's nearly impossible to persuade them otherwise.

I asked one woman, "Do you think you are a good person?"

"Oh, no," she answered quickly.

"So you've killed another person? Raped someone? Stolen a car?" I asked.

"No, of course not!"

"So what have you done that makes you a solidly bad person?"

"Well, because of being in treatment, I've cost my family a lot of money."

"And that makes you bad? Worthless?"

"Of course. I suppose I'll need to get better, then pay back the money to not be worthless."

It's like jumping a chasm for individuals like this one to begin to see that even though in this season of life they don't feel good about their behavior, they are more than these behaviors. Just as everything about them isn't good, everything about them isn't evil either.

We work together to try on new self-descriptors. I ask them to say: "I'm a good person; I try to do things in a loving way and not be hurtful. And (*not "but"*) I goof up sometimes. I'm a valuable person who sometimes does things wrong."

With one young woman who couldn't let go of self-condemnation for her choice to have premarital sex, I asked these questions:

"Are you choosing premarital sex as a way of life? Are you encouraging others to do it?"

"Of course not!" she replied. "You know I think it was a weak and stupid thing for me to do."

"So," I prodded gently, "Why can't you say, 'I made a decision at one point; it wasn't the healthiest for me. I've decided not to do that again. Here are the things I'm putting in place so I won't engage in that behavior in the future.'"

"How about saying 'I'm a good person who does stupid things sometimes. My self-esteem may go up and down, but when it goes down I can change things and bring it back up. Shifts in my self-esteem don't change my self-worth. I can behave badly and still be worthy of love. I still have value.'"

Leaving the doormat behind

As individuals break up with what may have been the major controllable relationship in their lives – their eating disorder – the desire, and the need for other relationships naturally presents itself.

The problem is, eating disorders were sometimes useful in keeping other people at bay. Why reach out when most relationships weren't reciprocal or balanced?

Here's a tool I use as the sufferer and I explore this question together.

I present a whiteboard and marker, and ask the individual to draw herself in the center. Then, around her, I ask that she draw symbols for others in her life – her parents, perhaps, and her friends – then any others who are important, like co-workers or siblings – anyone she considers significant.

Now the exercise gets interesting. I request that she connect herself to each of the others she's drawn with two arrows – one to represent how much she gives each person, and the second to represent how much that person (or persons) gives to her. If her arrow is larger, it means she's giving more; if the other person's is larger, it means he or she is giving more. We are trying to understand the balance or imbalance in her current relationships.

If the arrow analogy doesn't make sense, I say, "Imagine yourself as a bank account; these others in your life are bank accounts, too. Your arrow to them represents the times and ways they withdraw love, compassion, expertise or energy from you. Their arrow to you pictures how often you make these same withdrawals from them. Show me the flow between you – who is sending more; who is sending less?"

Most of the time, nearly all the bigger arrows are those from the person I'm working with to the others in her life. Indeed, it's not uncommon to see the arrows coming back toward her as pencil-thin, or non-existent.

In other words, she's a classic doormat. No balance. Little reciprocity. Her relationships are giver/taker, rescuer/victim, savior/sinker – with herself usually positioned in the giving role.

Then we talk about whether or not she's seen this before, and how it feels to her. What's good about that giver role? What does it provide in terms of self-protection, and control and power?

Independence vs. interdependence

I hear from some that the giver position makes sense, because they simply don't need anything from anyone else. Completely independent, that's them.

"Really?" I respond with amazement. "You filter your own water and grow your own food? And you manufacture your own car and refine your own gas – because I know you drove here. And you eat meat, so you must grow your own cows."

By now, they are often laughing as I say, "You'll have to help me understand how you are completely independent, because my life couldn't function without the help of a lot of other people."

Everyone needs relationships. Of course this truth plays out differently for each of us. Not everyone needs a thousand people in their lives, but there are those who thrive in a life crowded with others. For those with eating disorders, however, this is rarely true because relationships haven't proved to be a source of joy. They often feel abandoned and alone – for a number of reasons – so either avoiding others, or creating unbalanced relationships, seems like the only solution to the ache that comes from lacking positive relationships.

So, we back up. We talk about why balance matters in relationships, and what it might look like for her to experience more equal give-and-take with the people in her life.

Fears and anger surface quickly as disappointments and failed expectations come to light. I hear, "If I try to make it more even, I'll just get kicked around. I've asked for help before, and was ignored."

So the answer is evolution, not revolution; baby steps, not "one giant leap for mankind."

"Who might you be most comfortable beginning with?" I ask. "Who in this picture do you wish knew a little more about you? Who would feel safest to you to start with – maybe by inviting them to go for coffee, for instance, on a night when you know you are facing being alone?"

As she hems and haws, I sometimes say, "Do you want to pick, or do you want me to pick for you?" Clearly, I'm serious about this assignment.

Then I reassure her. "You don't need to open up all your pain to them! Just reach out and ask them to meet you instead of their coming first to you expecting your help. That's a start, right?"

Big steps grow from smaller ones

For some, reaching out is a bigger start than you might imagine.

This step is so large that sometimes when someone who has historically taken advantage of a person decides instead to be giving, often the person struggling will pull back, cancelling the opportunity. Being a receiver means experiencing vulnerability, and showing need – both fairly dangerous to one who has built a life on self-protection. So, moments like this allow us to move to another set of questions about resentments, anger, and disappointments, and about taking chances.

After this start we move to level two, relearning how to evaluate relationships, both for what they are, and what they could be. When an individual has taken a friend to dinner six times, but realizes that same friend showed no signs of concern when her grandmother died, questions arise.

First we ask, "Did your friend know you were sad? Could it be she would have responded differently if she had known?" Reasonable questions.

But if it's clear the friend did know, and did nothing, we talk about expectations for the relationship, and how to communicate these expectations without provoking defensiveness unnecessarily. We practice the words, like "I was hurt that I didn't hear from you when my grandmother died."

Not every relationship can be salvaged or renewed; some simply shouldn't be because there isn't adequate health on the other side to sustain genuinely reciprocal caring.

Our task in therapy is to help individuals understand their options, and know how to act on them. They can become better at communicating their needs, and at being willing to receive graciously when others reach out to meet those needs. Working on healthy communication is key to their recovery process.

When others don't respond, instead of withdrawing from the relationship, the person has the option of offering another opportunity through clearer communication of expectations. If they are then rejected, withdrawal might be the sensible and healthy next step.

Healthy relational boundaries open the way to the give-and-take between equals that make for genuine, safe intimacy. It generates trust that grows through caring and respect. The joy of shared love is one an eating disorder can never replicate.

Letting go of regrets and wrongs

Regrets about the past can keep those who struggle with eating disorders tied to that past.

My first marriage was a catastrophe by anyone's assessment. I felt like I had a scarlet letter, that no one would ever love me again. I had let God down and wasted my parents' money *again* paying for my wedding just after they'd recovered from the drain of my treatments.

But my mother said, "Brooke, the God I know is a forgiving God. I've been divorced. Am I awful? Do I have a scarlet letter?"

Ah, she had me there! Though I couldn't let myself off the hook, I knew she was wonderful. She cleverly pushed me to say, "If I conclude I'm a hopeless schmuck, I'll be saying that about Mom, too. And I know that's not true about her!" She provided a moment of deductive reasoning driven by love that saved me, allowed me to move on from a response to my mistake that could have formed my self-assessment for life.

My mom wasn't interested in justifying my mistake. She was simply naming it for what it was – a mistake – and giving me permission to learn from it, and move on with greater wisdom. And to reach out to others with compassion, perhaps helping them to avoid this same mistake.

Regrets for our bad choices, and resentment for wrongs done to us can both keep us imprisoned. For those with eating disorders, regrets and resentments can push them toward relapse as a way to find relief.

Letting go of trauma

The act of letting go is particularly challenging in the case of sexual abuse or rape. Some therapists push for forgiving the perpetrator as a way to find release.

I choose a different emphasis. I focus instead on taking back the power the abuser has tried to steal, and have seen huge shifts in thinking take place as a result.

One young woman worked with me to write a letter to her abuser. She chronicled what he had done to her, and how he had consequently held power over her. But then she wrote, "I will no longer let you control my health or my life. I deserve to be happy. I will no longer let you take that from me."

In trauma recovery terms, she was going back to remember the abuse, but then separating from it, and from the one who had administered it. Once a victim no longer sees herself as a helpless victim, then the role – and the strength – of the perpetrator must shift, too.

In this letting go of both regrets about my behavior and resentments about others' behavior, there often comes freedom to consider deeper questions.

Spirituality often moves naturally into our conversations because true recovery means living with hope. Hope comes from a sense of purpose, that my life isn't simply a random happenstance, and that I'm part of something larger than myself. When that's true, perhaps events in my life have happened for a reason, for purposes that are bigger and better than what I've understood so far.

Committing to health

Generating new ways to deal with life issues leads to rebuilding a life. That, in fact, is our purpose. If eating disorders persist because they distract us from dealing with deep pain, then we must, in time, find ways to lessen that pain so the distraction no longer makes sense.

I sometimes tell people, "At some point, you'll be healthy enough that when you face stress, you may still think about some of the destructive behaviors. *But they just won't seem worth it anymore.* It's not that you won't consider destructive behaviors; they won't make sense to you. Their price tag will become too high."

When I hear them tell me how they've found the price of illness just too high, I smile and tell myself, "One more monster, down for the count."

8

Validation and Redirection

One thing is likely clear by now: eating disorders appear to be all about food; in reality, they are all about emotions. Anxiety. Depression. Sadness. Shame. Guilt. Anger. Fear.

Over the long haul, the deep solutions to eating disorders rest in learning to expose and deal with emotions in healthy and life-giving ways. Health comes from changing – redirecting – emotional expressions away from harmful choices and toward healthy choices.

Sounds fairly simple, doesn't it? As a woman who nearly died from starvation, and had to be confined to a glass-walled room and threatened with feeding tubes in order to change, I'm telling you it's anything but simple.

Power tools

Two power tools made a deep, lasting, long-term difference for me. And I've seen the application of these two tools turn life around for other young people who suffer with eating disorders. Indeed, if I could gift every amazing person I work with these two tools, I think my therapy practice would soon close because there'd be no one needing my services.

What are these two power tools? Validation, and redirection.

1. Validation

The families of most of the individuals I work with do a great job supporting the expression of emotion, so long as that emotion is joy. Happiness, positivity, winning – all these feelings get lots of air space, and kudos all around.

However, joy, winning, positivity – these are just part of the complex fabric that makes up life. And feeling these things is only a portion of what makes us authentically and fully human. Life is light and dark, joy and sorrow, comfort and pain. It's the presence of each that makes its opposite richer.

But in many families – and I've seen this particularly with those whose children struggle with eating disorders – the dark side of life's emotions has no place.

One young women told me she'd never seen her parents express anger toward each other. Though I'm not an advocate of screaming matches in front of the children, this girl had no sense of what her own anger meant. Was there any room for anger in love? Or did feelings of anger toward another mean you didn't love them, or worse, they didn't love you?

Validating all emotions means we give them names – we label them – and we make room for them as normal and human.

Pictures of validation

Here's what I mean. When a child says, "I'm embarrassed," our parental, fix-it temptation is to jump in quickly to reassure. "Honey, that's silly," we say. "There's nothing to be embarrassed about."

Or maybe we jump quickly to shut down the negative expression because we don't want it – or where it might lead – to intrude in our world.

When a child says, "I don't like you, Mommy!" I can tell you from personal experience, it's very tempting to reprimand. "That is not the right way to feel about your mommy! And after all I do for you." (Am I the only parent out there who has entertained this reaction?)

However, we grow health when these uncomfortable emotions can come into the light of day, can be voiced and then acknowledged for what they are – simply feelings that are part of life. The danger comes when this validation doesn't happen, and a child learns that some things are okay to feel and say, and some aren't. When emotions can't be vetted, they buzz around inside like a swarm of angry bees shut up in a beehive, causing havoc inside.

"If I'm embarrassed it's silly," the child tells herself. "If I'm sad I need to suck it up and just move on. But I still feel what I feel. And now I also feel scared and alone – but I know I shouldn't say that, or I'll get another lecture."

Recently, a mom and her daughter sat together in my office, trying to understand the eating disorder that was consuming both their lives.

"Honey, I just want you to share with me what's going on," the mother pleaded with her daughter. "I do want to help."

The young woman looked at me, took a deep breath, and responded with candor that caught her mother off guard.

"Mom, I try to tell you stuff," she began. "I test the waters, but pretty quick I see it's not going to help to let you know what's really going on."

Her mother looked surprised, then confused. "Like when?"

"Like last week," the daughter said, "when I came out of my room and told you how overwhelmed I felt, and how I hadn't gotten any of my homework done. You freaked out. You said, 'Oh, my gosh! Why didn't you get your homework done? You're going to be so behind, and so overwhelmed this weekend!'"

Before her mother could interrupt, she went on. "Mom, I knew I was going to pay a price later. I was just trying to let you know how I was feeling. So, I'm not going to share other feelings with you if I see you can't manage a straight A student telling you she didn't get her homework finished one night."

The power of validation

There are moments when I have opportunity to help communi cation happen that might not otherwise; this would be one of them.

I turned to the mother. "What were your thoughts when you reacted to your daughter the way you did?" I asked.

"I wondered what I had done wrong. Obviously I'd dropped the ball. I should have asked her earlier what her homework was; I should be helping her with her homework!"

Note that in her response, Mom used the word "I" five times. Her reaction was less founded in disappointment toward her daughter than frustration with her failure to be whatever version of a great parent she had created for herself.

But her fifteen-year-old guessed none of this. She said to herself, "Mom is not responding to me. I tested the waters on a simple issue like homework, and it freaked her out. What if it was that I wanted to quit drill team? Or have sex with my boyfriend? Or... that I haven't eaten at all today?"

Validation and eating disorders

When I explain to families about the potential outcomes of "stuffing" conversations like the one you just overheard, they shake their heads in amazement.

"It happens like this," I tell them.

"Daughter decides she's going to have to keep things inside, because sharing her frustrations only generates greater frustration. Her feelings might have been normalized and managed with acceptance; instead they get stuffed and allowed to fester."

"Then, managing the growing discomfort inside can require restricting her food intake – the one thing she can control when feelings become too overwhelming. She can't manage her mother's or her teacher's or her coach's responses to her, but she can manage what goes into her body."

"So, she looks on pro-anorexia websites for ideas and support, anything to get control. There she finds girls boasting about not having eaten for say, three days, and challenging others to top their record. The young woman in trouble says, 'I can totally top that!' If she succeeds, unhealthy behaviors get cemented. If she fails she now tells herself, 'I'm not even a good anorexic,' and the downward spiral speeds up."

Self-doubt is part of all our lives; no one is immune. A girl who is not at-risk for emotional dysfunction will manage the moment and move through it.

An at-risk girl stays there, and makes uncomfortable feelings or thoughts a permanent part of her inner landscape. Instead of moving on, she moves away by engaging in compulsive behaviors that distract from the painful noise inside.

What validation sounds like

Validation isn't complex, but it is powerful. It simply means making words for what another seems to be feeling – and letting that person know that feeling is okay. It's normal. It's within the realm of human experience.

Here's what I mean. If the mom in my office had responded to her homework-deficient daughter in a validating way, she would have said, something light, "Honey, I get it. You're under a lot of stress right now. Homework must feel like just one more thing that's weighing on you. Is that right?"

Offering statements of acceptance can feel scary. "What if I'm giving permission for irresponsibility," we wonder to ourselves. "What if I'm teaching her to let moodiness or laziness control her life? Am I providing excuses so she can underperform…and fail in life?"

At moments like this, we need to look the possibilities straight in the eye. Honestly, what if this daughter didn't complete the homework, and her straight A average dropped a notch. In the long-haul that is life, will this event tank the possibility of a successful adult life? Is it going to ruin any chance for a successful career, or for love, or for happiness?

Even before I finish spelling out these dire options, some parents begin to sputter. "We want them to be all they can be. Right?"

We do, of course. But at what price? And if the young woman sitting with them is fighting for her life against an eating disorder, the price of this "be all you can be" prodding is too high.

When we make a place of safety for others to say out loud what they feel, and let them know by our response that those feelings are okay, we make a space for them to begin to manage those feelings toward healthier ends.

Learning to label emotions

Experiencing a strong emotion doesn't always mean we know how to label it. This is particularly true for kids. Understanding a name for what I'm feeling sometimes allows me to express it for what it is, rather than creating an inappropriate expression.

Parents can say, "I know you are so frustrated your brothers won't stay out of your room. I would feel like that, too. It doesn't mean it's going to change, but your feelings make sense." Or, "I think you were really embarrassed when I picked you up at school. What was going on?" Or, "It looks to me like you are in a hard place. Can you help me know where you are?"

This language may not be comfortable. I've had parents say, "For crying out loud! This is silly!" They believe their children should somehow automatically know how to name their emotions, so offering this kind of parental support feels artificial or unnecessary.

To these I say, "Give me a time when your daughter was really angry." And they might describe, say, an episode when she flew off the handle when it was time to go to bed. When they asked why she was mad, she said, "You told me it was time to take a shower, then I would have twenty minutes to play video games. But now you say it's time for bed."

Ah, perfect story for learning. "That's a great opportunity," I tell them, "to label and validate – something like, 'You felt like I forgot, that I was overlooking your time. You felt like that wasn't very fair.'"

Then I go a step farther. "And," I suggest, "You could also go on to say, 'Sweetie, I'm sorry. I forgot. It was my mistake.'"

This addendum is more agreeable to some parents than others. To those who see admitting mistakes as owning weakness, an apology only introduces hairline cracks into the granite statue of perfect parenting they are carving for themselves. But with an apology, I explain, we teach our kids that mistakes are okay. If we can make mistakes and apologize, they can, too. We make mistakes, we learn, we go on.

Validating without sacrificing authority

A few weeks ago unavoidable work demands meant I had to miss a class trip with my daughter. I explained and apologized more than once, but when my eight-year-old climbed into the car after that class trip day, I got pounded.

"*All* the parents were there," she wailed. "I was the *only one* alone…"

I'll confess, every defense mechanism in me leapt into action. "So, Katelyn, and Kylie, and Allison and Jillian – *all* of their parents were there?" Slowly, and one by one, she admitted that none of those parents attended.

Even though I do this work for a living, I'll admit it took several minutes for me to realize I had actually lost the only challenge that mattered. This conversation wasn't about whose data was more accurate; it was about an eight-year-old girl who wanted her mom to share a special day.

The more reasonable me took over, and I said, "Honey, I know you really wanted me there, and it upsets you when Mommy isn't on the trip. I wish I could have been with you today." And with this validation, she slowly moved past her anger.

As it turned out, we planned instead a special time together the following weekend. And though my clever little girl tried to suggest I "owed" her a special time, I made it clear I didn't, though I loved spending time with her and wanted more of it. She needed to know the world doesn't owe us; instead love chooses to give with joy.

I learned this response from my time in treatment at Cedar Ridge. On one occasion I went from home to Day Treatment wearing what I thought was a particularly cute outfit. Shorts were shorter than usual, worn with a brief tank top.

But when I arrived for the class, the leaders didn't agree. There were boys in treatment, too, and the leaders felt I was trying to expose my skinny body in ways that would win attention. (They were right, of course, though I never would have admitted this to them!)

They intervened at once, and made me replace that darling outfit with baggy scrubs for the day.

But along with the behavioral intervention, they also provided labeling and validation. "We know you think we are being ridiculous," they said to me – and of course I did, though I never voiced it. "And," they went on, "is there any part of you that is embarrassed about needing to change clothes?" Again, I was embarrassed, but at that time I had no words for these feelings.

Their response let me know they had expectations, but at the same time, I could feel anger and embarrassment, and still be okay. It was a great gift.

With labeling and validation, we aren't caving to our children's whims. We stand for what we believe is in their best interest. But we do it while at the same time receiving all of them – the good parts, and the not-so-good parts – in ways that help them know they don't have to starve themselves to manage life.

2. Redirection

Along with validation, redirection is the second life skill I would bequeath to all I work with if I could. If validation is the gift that helps manage emotions, redirection is the gift that helps manage behaviors.

Recovery from an eating disorder is less about stopping hurtful behaviors, and more about learning to choose healthier behaviors. It's about finding ways to feel and live life that lead to wholeness rather than illness. It's about redirection.

Redirection isn't an unfamiliar skill. If I notice all of my daughter's friends are gathering on the front porch, and she's holed up in her room, I say, "Honey, why don't you go outside for a while? You need some sun!" I don't move into a major psychotherapy moment; I simply offer the option of a different behavior than the one she's currently choosing.

In the context of a young person involved in hurtful behaviors, I coach parents in redirection, not as a way to control their child's behavior, but rather as an offering of support to help the young person learn to redirect herself.

Here's an example.

A mom whose teenager is bingeing and purging sees the girl headed to the pantry. So, the mother might ask the girl if she'd like to go for a walk. Or she might say, "Honey, I know you are bored right now. Would you like to help me with dinner?"

Or, "How about if you take your brothers to basketball with me so I don't have to drive alone?" Or, she might ask, "Have you talked to your best friend today?"

This young woman knows her mom is trying to jump in front of her behaviors and offer an alternative. Her intention is to help support the change her daughter wants to make, and to do it without shaming her.

In therapy we work diligently to offer new choices for times when emotions get overwhelming, things like journaling, or yoga, or music, or reaching out to others.

In other words, we're teaching people to redirect themselves. Until that habit becomes strong, supportive redirection from others can keep change moving.

Living monster-free

Eating disorders can kill, but as we've seen they don't have to. Moving through an eating disorder to recovery can both save a life, and make a life.

I've found my greatest strengths in the lessons I learned through dealing with an eating disorder. What came to my life to destroy me became the path to life for others and myself.

PART THREE:

A Health Focused Future

9

Life Beyond Eating Disorders

When it comes to body image and food, our culture has created a state of constant confusion.

Two television ads in a row tout the glories of thick-crusted, cheese and meat-laden pizza, followed by two ads for diet centers. A talk show announces the latest "medical break-through" to melt away your fat, then follows that segment with a cooking class for a decadent chocolate cake. This week protein is in; next week it's a contributor to kidney damage, and is a health hazard.

Honestly, what are we to think? No wonder I'm so often asked, "What does healthy look like, especially when it comes to food?"

Living healthy

I tell those I work with there are four mandates for healthy living I have relied on for these thirteen years since I moved to recovery from an eating disorder. They are these:

- Use food to nourish your body, no more.
- See coping skills as useful bridges.
- Trust your body to guide you.
- Remember no one does this alone.

1. Use food to nourish your body, no more.

One major commonality between those who struggle with anorexia and bulimia is this: both have stopped listening to their body signals about food. Eating becomes something other than a way to satisfy simple hunger. Rather, it becomes an (unproductive) answer to other kinds of questions food was never intended to address.

For example, if an individual has just had a fairly balanced dinner, and an hour later feels driven to consume a quart of ice cream, I wonder if something else is going on. Is she really physically unsatisfied, or is there an unpleasant emotion poking its way into her consciousness, and the ice cream is providing a welcome distraction.

When hunger cues are associated with emotion, we work to separate the two. As a teaching tool, we encourage people to eat in a regular rhythm, say about 6 times a day. If their food intake is sufficient, this rhythm should keep their blood sugar level, their bodies nourished, and hunger at bay.

Then, if they feel compulsions to eat more or more frequently, we ask them to monitor emotions. Was there boredom? Loneliness? Another feeling that isn't comfortable?

Once some of these feelings have names, we find ways to deal with them for what they are, with more effective, and less harmful tools than potato chips.

The use of the HALT acronym often makes this emotional awareness easier to understand. Are you Hungry, Angry, Lonely or Tired? If you are truly hungry, then food makes a difference. But anger, loneliness and fatigue don't respond to food; there are better solutions.

One individual I work with has posted the HALT reminder on her fridge. Then, when she feels compelled to engage in behaviors, she works to identify which of the four she is actually feeling, and then attempts to wait 20 minutes before engaging. That period is often long enough to find another intervention for anger, loneliness or tiredness – one that actually creates emotional improvement in a way food never could.

2. See coping skills as useful bridges.

We've talked a lot in previous chapters about coping skills – about redirecting when a compulsion to over exercise presents itself, or finding new ways to respond to the urge to rescue. Developing coping skills is a key part of recovery.

For example, one young woman told me, "I have the serenity prayer posted in my car, but I still turn into Wendy's for a burger and fries even though I've already eaten."

I asked, "When you see the serenity prayer, what would happen if you started saying it? If you repeated it out loud until you are at your destination?" The next day she reported, "I said the serenity prayer all the way to Topeka!" One day down. That's success.

But this success doesn't mean that in order to live healthy she'll need to repeat the serenity prayer over and over for the rest of her life. The coping skill – focusing on the positive thoughts instead of on food – is a bridge. It's a practical, accessible way to break an older pattern so a new one has a chance to emerge, first as a trial, then as a permanent part of life.

The process of recovery from an eating disorder is slow; there is no quick fix because recovery means restructuring how we do life. Learning and adding new skills learning takes time.

Coping skills are bridges between destructive behaviors and healthy living. In time, the coping skills simply won't be needed anymore, but during recovery time they can help movement away from illness. So, I encourage those I work with to apply the skills diligently, while recognizing a different way of living solidly in view.

3. Trust your body to guide you

Healthy eating means listening to your body, eating when you are hungry, stopping before you are too full, eating variety. Simple as that.

If we settle into listening to what our body wants, it won't always tell us to head to a Mexican restaurant for a huge combo plate, as some fear. During the holiday party season, I was offered dips and sweets and heavy foods repeatedly – and in general, I eat what's offered. When I got ready to come back to work after the holidays, all I could think about was a kale salad. My body was telling me I needed the vegetables.

And remember, this message was coming from a person who once starved herself to 70% of ideal body weight and honestly believed that a bit of ranch dressing on my arm would some-how increase the size of my behind. If I can learn to listen to my body, and trust it will guide me to good choices, anyone can.

The alternative to listening and trusting is getting caught up in all the food and dieting chaos around us.

If you wonder if it's wise to trust your body, then try to convince yourself it's far wiser to trust the messages of a culture that one day insists eggs are evil *(all that cholesterol!)* and the next decides it's the food of choice *(pure protein!)* I submit y you would be better off listening to your body.

Of course it may take some retraining for our bodies to speak accurately. For example, our bodies need to wake up in the morning to be able to send reasonable signals about hunger and fullness through the day. So, I suggesting startiing the day with a protein and carbohydrate combination – cereal and milk, or a piece of cheese and a bagel, perhaps.

Eating first thing like this often awakens a sense of hunger by 10:30 or 11:30, when a small around of food will satisfy. Those who don't eat breakfast don't start their bodies' engines, and won't feel hunger pangs until 1 or 2 in the afternoon. Then, when hunger signals do turn on, overeating often results.

The body cues can be trusted if we give ourselves what we need to activate them accurately.

4. Remember no one does this alone.

For those I work with, trust is a four-letter word. The kinds of off-kilter thinking that leads to eating disorders also convinces we can't depend on anyone's love or help, so trust will only lead to disappointment.

But as we heal, wise and careful trust can become not just resource, but joy.

Of course I'm not describing the blind trust that believes everyone and everything – I've learned the hard way to take great care in choosing who I lean on. But there are trustworthy others in the world, and learning to depend on them – and to allow them to depend on you, too – opens a door to long-term strength and resilience.

Life as part of a healthy culture

We've spent considerable time talking personally about behaviors and changing them in order to put food, weight and shape in their proper place.

Some of these challenges would be lessened if we lived in a culture where the messages we receive are more congruent with health than with illness.

There are two messages I would especially like to change, if I ruled the world. They have to do with our understanding of how we measure health, and our understanding of how we measure worth.

1. A healthy culture measures health accurately

We've come to claim something called the BMI – the body mass index – as the source of absolute truth when it comes to health. And as measured by BMI standards, one-third the people in our country are overweight. Many of these are now beginning to pay the price of this judgment in insurance premiums, in hiring choices, and in social acceptability.

But let me offer a counterpoint from my personal life for your consideration.

My husband is simply a large man, tall, big, muscular and athletic. He has good cholesterol numbers; his heart is healthy. If you met him, you'd say, "Who on earth would diagnose this man as obese?"

Yet per the BMI targets our insurance company utilizes, Scott has been declared obese.

There's no accounting for variables like bone structure, muscle mass, or any other determinants. So, as a result, anyone 5'5" and 165 lbs. is clinically obese. But we work with athletes who don't fit these definitions. A 5'5" college soccer player shouldn't weigh 125 pounds – he'll look emaciated.

A friend of mine is two inches taller than me, yet her wrist is half the size of mine. She's not an athlete, so her muscle mass isn't great.

Is she anorexic? I can verify she isn't; I know her eating habits well, and frankly, by this time, I'm pretty tough to fool! But she is simply genuinely small-boned. Another friend of ours is nearly the same height, and weighs 150. I fall between the two of these on the scale, yet the three of us wear the same clothing size, handy since we can trade black tie event dresses to save stress on our clothing budgets.

Two of the three of us doesn't fit the range mandated by the BMI for good health. I ask then, who's actually unhealthy? My friends, or those who've decided that the BMI will be our absolute standard of what's right to weigh?

Here's the issue I see with this – besides undeserved increases in insurance premiums for some. When doctors, or insurance companies, or the media lay unrealistic expectations on us, shame can result. And offices like mine are filled with men and woman who have gotten in trouble seeking fast-acting solutions to rid them of shame. Now they are drawn to clinics that provide HCG shots, or weight-loss hormones, or no-carb solutions to drop pounds overnight. But the result of the quick solutions is damage to metabolism, and in the end, greater heaviness and more resistance to weight loss by reasonable means.

A colleague from the world of eating disorders warned about the dangers of quick-fix solutions, and got aggressive pushback from a nurse listening.

"You are telling kids – even overweight kids – they don't need to lose weight?" she asked, incredulous.

"I am promoting balance," my colleague replied, "not numbers on a scale. If we are doing the things our bodies are made to do – moving, stopping eating before we are stuffed, then kids will be okay."

"But I know for a fact that diets work!" the nurse argued.

"How do you know?" my colleague queried.

"I know because I've been on [a popular commercial diet plan] *six times* – and I lost weight *every time!*"

Really? If these diet programs work to create successful, permanent weight loss, why would anyone need to go back six times?

But the greater danger from my view is this. If you follow these popular diet plans and are "successful" losing weight, then later you regain the weight, who do you blame?

Do you fault the diet company because their idea of quick weight loss isn't a healthy approach? Or do you fault yourself for lack of will power, or food addiction or laziness? I submit we lay shame on ourselves for lack of discipline – and others do, as well. The weight loss program comes away unsmudged; we come away condemned.

Shame is not a powerful driver to good health, though I see daily that it does a great job driving people to harmful behaviors that put their health at risk.

Every man at 6'1" does not need to weigh 190-210 pounds. Every 5'5" tall woman who weighs 150 is not obese. If we could abandon – or at least refine – our measure of health, I believe the goal of genuine health would be more attainable for more of us.

2. A healthy culture measures worth accurately

We are human *beings*, not human *doings*.

Yet, what happens if we hit a day when none of our friends call, or our spouse needs nothing from us, or work demands nothing? Perhaps for a short while it felt relieving, but then, an uneasy feeling starts to gnaw at us, as if without these things, there might be nothing left.

Can we let go of the pressure to produce, and simply be content. Can we be okay with our own thoughts and not have to be producing something to have value?

We live in a culture that starts this "you are how much you do" pressure early. Our children don't get invited to a birthday party, so they feel shame. Or their friends are off to piano lessons, or soccer practice, or religion class, while they sit with the family having dinner. And they ask, "Why are they doing more than me? Am I missing out?"

Our teens live with a greater pressure. A teacher may push them toward AP classes; another informs them that without a 36 on the ACT there won't be college scholarships; or, reminds a great student that a 4.7 GPA instead of "just" a 4.0 would look great on college applications. It also helps if you are doing volunteer work, are a member of the National Honor Society, and of course, are on an athletic team.

Because of my own over-functioning nature, and the over-functioning young men and women I work with daily, I'm on a Being Crusade.

For starters, I don't let my kids do more than one activity at a time. One wants to play the violin – wonderful! And she also wants to ride horses. "You need to choose," I tell her. "We aren't going to do both."

But the last time I said no to my son playing both baseball and soccer, other parents tried to step in. "The two activities only overlap by three weeks," they pushed me. He could ride to practice with us."

I work on pushing myself into more being, too. Like the days when I turn off my phone and computer in order to be more present for my kids. Or when I make the choice not to immediately return a call because my husband has asked me to enjoy a basketball game with him.

As an inexperienced therapist, I felt compelled to respond to everyone's request immediately. But as I matured, I learned that some of these responses had more to do with my own overblown sense of importance and my own need to validate my worth than they did what was best for those I worked with.

Actually, part of my job is to help individuals learn that I am not the source of all their health; they have the capacity to resolve their own crises. If I'm always there to fix things, there's no need to develop inner resources of their own. This understanding marked some of my own movement away from a life of a doing toward a life more being-focused.

Choices like this require being secure in your own decisions. It takes strength to not allow others to make our decisions. So, just as I ask others to do, I now do periodic checks of my own values – which are most important to me? Then I put those values against how I'm spending my time to be sure I'm putting my money where my mouth is about doing vs. being.

Creating a picture of recovery

Toward the end of the recovery process, I often ask people to draw a picture of their understanding of what recovery means, understanding this will mean something different for each person.

One young woman pictured herself as an apple tree. Growing beautifully on that tree were beautiful, red apples labeled honesty, respect, friends, family, self-expression, positivity, hard work, and happiness.

Beneath the tree, on the ground, lay apples labeled heartbreak, depression, negative thoughts, and loss.

"Life for me now," she told me, "is about throwing out more and more of those bad apples so more of the good ones have room to flourish."

I smiled, and thought of the way a friend of mine describes her process of recovery. "It takes time," she said. "And it definitely is a process. First I felt like I was climbing a mountain. Then the mountain became hills to climb. Now life is more like walking on a plateau with some speed bumps along the way."

Good apples over rotten ones? Speed bumps instead of mountains? Either word picture works; both tell a story of how life can turn from devastation to radiance.

I've seen it happen for me, and now for hundreds of young women and men who believed an eating disorder would be the end of them. Instead of ending their lives, facing and overcoming that disorder has given them strength and courage that radiates from their lives.

It's not perfection we are experiencing, but the freedom to be imperfect human beings sure enough of our own worth that we no longer need unhealthy distractions to shield us from life.

Closing Thoughts from Brooke

As you struggle with an eating disorder, do you sometimes wonder what your future might be? Let me tell you about mine.

My life today is filled with faith, family, joy, peace, work and continued learning. The eating disorder chapter we've explored together has been closed for roughly thirteen years; I enjoy life now as mother, wife, friend, therapist, business owner and athlete. I believe that my obsession with weight, shape and food is behind me, though I always remain aware of the dark places it took me, and the challenging journey back to health. I am not blind to the bumps in the road that may come, but feel confidant that I will be able to manage them safely.

Now, when I think back to the battle with anorexia, I can even see gifts that came from the fight. I have learned to relax, play, set boundaries, embrace my flaws, and notice my strengths in ways I wouldn't have if these struggles had never happened.

Most importantly, I relish my children differently because I once feared I'd lost the chance for successful pregnancies. I hold dear a marriage where I feel honored, because I know intimately what disrespect and disregard feel like. And I feel privileged to be part a profession that allows me to work with so many amazing individuals, both through professional and therapeutic relationships, because I know this journey to health from both sides.

My life isn't perfect, but now I know it doesn't have to be struggle-free – and I don't have to be struggle-free – for every day to be filled with meaning.

In my work over the past ten years, I have heard so many women and men say that they don't feel like they have a purpose. My response is this: what if **being** is your purpose for today? What if learning from this experience is what you **can do** in this moment?

When I offer this challenge, I smile, because I recall the time when how much I was worth came from how much I did. And I give thanks that discovering the power of being has set me free.

So, this is what I believe about me. Now, may I tell you what I believe about you?

I believe you are here for a reason, and every life experience is serving a good purpose.

I believe you are learning transformational lessons that will make you strong, even though you feel punished, defeated and burdening to others.

I believe the eating disorder that plagues you doesn't define you. It is a temporary costume -- a mask that is hiding all that you can become.

So, please. Fight the eating disorder with all of the tools that we discussed. You can break free. I know you can heal.

Thank you for your time. You've honored me in your choice to read this book. Now I honor you for your determination to seek – and keep on seeking – until radiant health and wholeness is yours.

.

Recommended Reading

If you struggle with an eating disorder, or love someone who does, you may enjoy these resources:

Boundaries: When to Say Yes, When to Say No to Take Control of Your Life. Henry Cloud and John Townsend (Zondervan, 1992)

Intuitive Eating: A Recovery Book for the Chronic Dieter. Evelyn Tribole and Elyse Resch (St. Martin's Paperbacks, 1996)

Succulent Wild Women: Dancing with Your Wonder-Full Self. SARK (Touchstone, 1997)

Big Fat Lies Women Tell Themselves: Ditch Your Inner Critic and Wake Up Your Inner Superstar. Amy Ahlers and SARK (New World Library, 2011)

To learn more about therapeutic approaches:

Cognitive Behavioral Therapy and Eating Disorders, Christopher G. Fairburn (The Guilford Press, 2008).

ABOUT THE AUTHOR

Brooke Wesley is a LSCSW (Licensed Specialist Clinical Social Worker) who received her Bachelor's Degree in Psychology and Master's Degree in Social Work from the University of Missouri Kansas City. She has worked as a therapist in a variety of settings since completing her formal training in 2000.

Brooke has worked with adolescents and adults who struggle with eating disorders, substance abuse, depression, anxiety disorders, self-harm behaviors and personality disorders. Working in a high school setting for several years motivated Brooke to advocate for students, while teaming with the education system to create a safe environment for teens to learn and grow.

Brooke is passionate about the whole person, introducing strengths-based methods and positive, healthy coping skills to those she works with. In addition to individual and group counseling, Brooke is co-founder of Thalia House, and speaks publicly on a variety of mental health issues.

At Thalia House, we recognize eating disorder recovery is a journey requiring ongoing support. For many young women, a supportive transition from inpatient or residential treatment to their home environment is essential to prevent relapse. For other young women, recovery requires more structure and support in daily living than outpatient therapy alone.

Thalia House is for young women who are able to live independently and desire the support of a recovery community as they practice life skills and gain freedom from their eating disorder. Residents take responsibility for living a healthy lifestyle while receiving guidance from our staff and support from their peers. Each resident establishes goals for the future and becomes involved in part-time employment, school, and/or volunteer work during her stay at Thalia House.

You can learn more at thaliahouse.com.